The Computer Guy
Guy
Is Here!

The Mainframe Mechanic

By John C. Sak
CE, MM (Retired)

The Computer Guy is Here!

ISBN: 1545083177
ISBN-13: 978-1545083178

Contents

Contents

Introduction

Way back in the last century, back in the 1960s, computers were mammoth mysterious machines. They were immensely expensive machines. Large companies depended on these machines every day to keep their businesses running. Yet, no one saw them. They were securely tucked away in environmentally controlled rooms. Only their operators were allowed access. These were the people who actually made the computer do the work. On the other hand, these well trained operators knew nothing of the secrets behind the covers. If a problem arose, there was no choice but to call the computer guy. He was the one who knew what secrets lay behind those closed doors.

Whenever a problem reared its ugly head, a supervisor franticly placed a call for service and then waited. And waited. There was little to do without the computer running. Finally someone would yell out, "The computer guy is here!"

The computer guy was warmly greeted by the thankful supervisor… who immediately wanted to know how long it would take to fix the problem. So, with everyone looking over his shoulder, the computer guy set about his business determining the problem and finding a solution.

Well, that's just the beginning of the story.

* * * * *

Who were these guys? Where did they come from? Exactly what did they do? What the heck is a Mainframe Mechanic? And finally, what happened to them? This book will answer all those questions. It will also add insight into the daily lives of those involved back in the Mainframe Computer Era. Along the way you will find much additional information to enable an understanding of that era. And the journey even includes numerous odd bits of computer history.

Background

Early large-scale computers from the 1960s until sometime in the 1990s were known as mainframe computers. The name comes from the fact that those computers were composed of many interconnected machines, called frames. Multiple frames were necessary for a computing system to function. Most of the frames contained supporting equipment like input and output devices, various storage devices for data and so on. Only one of those frames was the actual computer, the Central Processing Unit. This was the *main* frame of the computer system.

Each of the frames contained far more than just electronic circuits. They also contained power supplies, receptacles for connecting the frames together and cooling equipment. In fact, many old mainframe computers produced so much heat they required water cooling. They were actually connected to city water supplies! And, last but not least, there was a need to communicate with the computer. Back then, the operator used a modified electric typewriter to talk to the computer system.

Much of this machinery was mechanical rather than electronic. Input and output devices, such as printers and machines to read and punch data cards were almost entirely mechanical but were controlled electronically.

Although the Computer Operator was the most visible of the human beings running a computer, many other people were required to keep things humming. Computers required programmers working behind the scenes to create the sets of computer instructions known as programs. Programs were always written for very specific uses or applications. The applications included things like payroll or accounts receivable or parts inventory. Currently the term computer program has been replaced by the term "app" which sounds friendly and far less technical. Whichever term is used, they still require skilled practitioners in the art of programming.

There was also a need for Data Librarians, Tape Handlers, Schedulers and many others who all worked together to assure a smooth operational flow. And we'd better not forget about the Management team.

That computer guy was not often seen and little has been written about him. Still he was part of that small army of people who were needed to ensure a smooth running system. The computer guy was actually a Field Engineer and he worked for the computer company, not the computer user.

Rather than design things as do most engineers, Field Engineers worked to install, maintain and improve the machines and systems. Whenever a computer component failed, it was this computer guy who fixed the problem. Field Engineers were also responsible for documenting the cause of each failure and helping in the design of improvements that would eliminate future failures. That was a key part of the Field Engineering job.

When a computer system broke down, it was obviously a bit more complicated than changing a light bulb. But electronic circuits seldom failed. The truth of the matter is that the vast majority of computer system problems were failures involving the mechanical portions of the system. Field Engineers were most often called upon to exercise their mechanical knowledge and skills. Occasionally they were even plumbers when a cooling system component failed. Because of the relative frequency of using those various skills, Field Engineers often referred to themselves as computer mechanics or more specifically as mainframe mechanics.

* * * * *

Around 1966, IBM decided to change the job title of its Field Engineers to Customer Engineers. Supposedly customers would be comforted knowing these engineers were on hand just for them. A token or marketing ploy? Perhaps. But in a way it made sense. Field Engineers, or now Customer Engineers, spent almost all their time at customer locations. Their main objective was to keep customers happy by maintaining the computer systems at a high level of availability.

Customer Engineers, CEs for short, were involved in all aspects of a computer system, not just troubleshooting and repairing problems. CEs did everything from helping in the planning of a computer system to actually installing the machines that made up the system. They performed periodic maintenance, diagnostic testing, updating of hardware and software and frequently upgraded the systems.

While the following relies mostly on the experiences of one CE and those he knew, it is really the story of any Customer Engineer. It is

3

an insight into the era of mainframe computing through the experiences of real mainframe mechanics.

Most every old Field Engineer/Customer Engineer has, at one time or another, thought (and occasionally said) "I could tell you stories..." Well, this old CE finally decided to put some of them to paper.

1 - Beginnings

A machine that could calculate faster than a man had been the goal of mathematicians and scientists for centuries. Yet a truly usable computing machine had always been held back by technology. Wheels, gears and mechanical complexity were obvious impediments.

The electronic age brought the speed of light (electrons) into play. That was a major breakthrough. At first vacuum tubes were used to solve the speed and mechanical problems, but they created a different problem. There was speed, but now there was also heat. The hundreds of vacuum tubes necessary to create a computer produced a tremendous amount of heat. Furthermore, like a light bulb, vacuum tubes had glowing filaments that frequently burned out.

Invention of the transistor in 1947 was a gigantic leap in technology. But like any new technology, there were also limitations. These tiny electronic switches could not handle large amounts of power. Also they were very sensitive to heat. Those problems, and others, required solving before a practical device could be produced. Enough of those issues were solved to allow the first pocket transistor radio to appear in 1953. The first silicon based transistors came a year later. This allowed greater power handling capabilities. Other improvements came with increasing speed.

Only five years after the silicon based transistor was invented, IBM announced the first commercially available all transistor computer. No longer did a computer occupy huge rooms full of hot vacuum tubes. The IBM 1400 Computing System was more like an appliance store's refrigerator section. This ushered in the computer Mainframe Era, generally recognized as beginning in 1960.

Four years further down the road, IBM introduced their System 360 which utilized integrated circuits, the next technological advance. The pace of technological advances continued. By 1976, "the Steves", Jobs and Wozniak, began marketing a computer that literally fit on top of a desk. By no means could it replace the big mainframe computers, but these guys sure started something. By the time IBM finally

5

introduced its own personal computer in 1981, there were already a dozen major companies making breadbox size computers.

Steve Jobs & Steve Wozniak, founders of Apple Computing

A moment in time

The era of the mainframe computers was rather brief, lasting not much more than 30 years. But not only was it a time of evolution and revolution, it was a time of innovation and continual improvement. There was constant, relentless change for the entire period. If one factor among the myriad of changes could be singled out as definitive, it would have to be the continuous shrinking of electronic circuits.

In 1965, Gordon Moore of Fairchild Semiconductor Corp. made a prediction that eventually became known as Moore's Law. He predicted that semiconductor devices, (transistors, integrated circuits and the like) would shrink to HALF their size each year for the foreseeable future. That law seems to be holding even today. Where a mainframe computer had once filled a room larger than most houses, today literally hundreds of computers fit comfortably in a standard 19" wide electronics equipment rack. Computers with mainframe power shrunk to the size of a desk. Computers then shrunk to fit on top of a desk. Soon they were balancing on peoples knees. Now they are super thin tablets you can carry under your arm like a newspaper. Even cell phones contain much computing power.

The era of mainframe computers began shortly before this author's involvement, yet it did not last the length of his career. It was a very short period of time that could be compared to that of the "barnstorming era" following WWI. Before that war to end all wars, aircraft were rare and extremely expensive. Following The Great War the excess of war birds meant surplus prices. Hundreds of adventurers took to the skies. Like that brief era, the mainframe computer era was anything but dull and uneventful. It was short, but filled with wonder, intrigue, freedom and satisfaction. There was even humor and a sense of fulfillment in those who experienced it.

Although this is not a history of the era, we have included some interesting bits of history along the way. Admittedly some people may see it as geek history, but so be it.

What We All Saw

Computers had, in a limited way, been around since World War II, but the available technology kept them hidden away in mysterious buildings. Through 1960, few people had ever seen a computer. Technological advances began shrinking computers to where they now fit in rooms smaller than a house. Computers finally began appearing on television. We saw a stack of punched cards disappearing into the bowels of a machine. We saw spinning reels. By the mid-1960s, most people thought they had finally seen a real computer. We can thank the TV news folks for those images. But the truth was most people still had not seen a computer.

After all, computers are calculating machines, not moving assembly lines or amusement rides. Actually computers are downright boring. You can't see the electrons doing their thing. The only indication that something was happening came from rows of light bulbs, as they blinked on and off. Rows of tiny blinking light bulbs were just not impressive enough for the nightly news. Since television is a visual media, the TV producers wanted action. Real action. The only parts of a computer system that satisfied that need were the tape drives or card reading machines or perhaps the output printers. Producers were even known to implore the computer operators to make the tape reels move faster. The public still had not really seen a computer.

Input

The basic input for a computer in the 1950s and 1960s was the iconic 3-1/4" by 7-3/8" piece of stiff paper known as an IBM Card. IBM and their customers called them that, but the competition preferred the term "punched card." The idea of using punched holes to represent information was not new to the computer era. In fact, the whole concept goes back to the 18th Century where wooden or heavy cardboard "cards" were used to control weaving looms made by companies like Bouchon and Jacquard.

Probably the most famous early use of the punched card principle was in the US Census of 1890. The previous US Census had taken an astounding 7 years to complete. As the country continued to grow it was obvious something had to be done to speed the process.

Enter Herman Hollerith to save the day. This son of German immigrants was the proud holder of an Engineer of Mines degree from Columbia University (specialized in geology and math). I know that degree doesn't make much sense today, but it's a fact. He invented a system to mechanically speed the census process. This included a method of encoding numbers and alphabetic characters as a pattern of holes in heavy paper cards. He also designed a machine he called a tabulating machine that could read those codes and calculate totals. As a bonus, the information on the punched cards could be reused for double checking a total or for additional calculations at some later date.

Hollerith's coding was simple but effective. Each number or character was punched into one column on the card. Each column contained 12 rows. The lower 10 rows were for the numbers 0 thru 9. The top 2 rows, he named X and Y, represented a binary code to define alphabetic characters. As the result, each column could represent one of 40 different characters and a number of special characters too. The number of columns per card varied over the years but was finally standardized at 80 columns per card in 1928. Hollerith's code and the 80 column cards stood the test of time.

```
&-0123456789 ABCDEFGHIJKLMNOPQR/STUVWXYZ #@ .< $* ,%
 ▮         ▮▮▮▮▮▮▮▮▮                  ▮▮
 ▮              ▮▮▮▮▮▮▮▮▮              ▮▮
0 0 0▮0 0 0 0 0 0 0 0 0 0 0 0 0 0 0 0 0 0 0 0 0 0 0 0 0 0 0 0 0▮▮▮▮▮▮▮▮▮▮0 0 0 0 0 0 0 0 0▮▮0 0 0 0 0 0 0 0 0 0 0 0 0 0 0 0 0 0 0 0 0 0 0 0 0 0 0
1 1 1 1▮1 1 1 1 1 1 1 1▮1 1 1 1 1 1 1 1▮1 1 1 1 1 1 1 1▮1 1 1 1 1 1 1 1 1 1 1 1 1 1 1 1 1 1 1 1 1 1 1 1 1 1 1 1 1 1 1 1 1 1 1 1 1 1 1 1 1 1 1 1 1 1
2 2 2 2 2▮2 2 2 2 2 2 2 2▮2 2 2 2 2 2 2 2▮2 2 2 2 2 2 2 2▮2 2 2 2 2 2 2 2 2 2 2 2 2 2 2 2 2 2 2 2 2 2 2 2 2 2 2 2 2 2 2 2 2 2 2 2 2 2 2 2 2 2 2 2 2 2
3 3 3 3 3 3▮3 3 3 3 3 3 3 3▮3 3 3 3 3 3 3 3▮3 3 3 3 3 3 3 3▮3 3 3 3 3 3 3▮3 3▮3 3▮3 3▮3 3 3 3 3 3 3 3 3 3 3 3 3 3 3 3 3 3 3 3 3 3 3 3 3 3 3 3 3 3
4 4 4 4 4 4 4▮4 4 4 4 4 4 4 4▮4 4 4 4 4 4 4 4▮4 4 4 4 4 4 4 4▮4 4 4 4 4 4 4▮4 4▮4 4▮4 4▮4 4 4 4 4 4 4 4 4 4 4 4 4 4 4 4 4 4 4 4 4 4 4 4 4 4 4 4 4
5 5 5 5 5 5 5 5▮5 5 5 5 5 5 5 5▮5 5 5 5 5 5 5 5▮5 5 5 5 5 5 5 5▮5 5 5 5 5 5 5 5 5 5 5 5 5 5 5 5 5 5 5 5 5 5 5 5 5 5 5 5 5 5 5 5 5 5 5 5 5 5 5 5
6 6 6 6 6 6 6 6 6▮6 6 6 6 6 6 6 6▮6 6 6 6 6 6 6 6▮6 6 6 6 6 6 6 6▮6 6 6 6 6 6 6 6 6 6 6 6 6 6 6 6 6 6 6 6 6 6 6 6 6 6 6 6 6 6 6 6 6 6 6 6 6 6 6 6
7 7 7 7 7 7 7 7 7 7▮7 7 7 7 7 7 7 7▮7 7 7 7 7 7 7 7▮7 7 7 7 7 7 7 7▮7 7 7 7 7 7 7 7 7 7 7 7 7 7 7 7 7 7 7 7 7 7 7 7 7 7 7 7 7 7 7 7 7 7 7 7 7 7 7 7
8 8 8 8 8 8 8 8 8 8 8▮8 8 8 8 8 8 8 8▮8 8 8 8 8 8 8 8▮8 8 8 8 8 8 8 8▮8 8▮▮8▮▮8▮▮8▮▮8 8 8 8 8 8 8 8 8 8 8 8 8 8 8 8 8 8 8 8 8 8 8 8 8 8 8 8 8 8
9 9 9 9 9 9 9 9 9 9 9▮9 9 9 9 9 9 9 9▮9 9 9 9 9 9 9 9▮9 9 9 9 9 9 9 9▮9 9 9 9 9 9 9 9 9 9 9 9 9 9 9 9 9 9 9 9 9 9 9 9 9 9 9 9 9 9 9 9 9 9 9 9 9 9
```

An 80 column card punched with the Hollerith Code

So how did these cards become known as IBM cards? Following his work for the Census Bureau, Hollerith went on to teach at the prestigious Massachusetts Institute of Technology. During his time at MIT, he continued to refine his tabulating system. Eventually he formed a company to build his tabulating machines. Appropriately, he named it The Tabulating Machine Company. His company prospered and in 1911, he merged with two other companies to form The Computing-Tabulating-Recording Company. The C-T-R Company grew enough to open a Canadian subsidiary, which was named the International Business Machine Company. That seemed an obvious name choice since the business had crossed the northern border. The Computing-Tabulating-Recording Company, despite its unwieldy name, continued to grow. Finally, in 1924, then C-T-R President, Thomas J. Watson Sr. decided to rename the entire company the International Business Machines Corporation. The name now reflected the true nature of the entire company.

* * * * *

I was once asked why the IBM card was such an unusual size. Why wasn't it 4" x 8" or some other more common size? Believe it or not, the size is tied to US currency. In 1929, US currency was standardized to its current format. But prior to that, banknotes, currency certificates, dollar bills, etc. came in several different sizes. For reasons known only to Herman Hollerith, the old large currency format was chosen for his punch cards. That 3-1/4" x 7-5/8" format continued with IBM because it was far easier than redesigning all their machines to accommodate a different size.

Also, people have inquired as to why the upper left corner of the card is usually cut off. Hollerith's system calls for columns to be numbered from left to right with bottom row representing nine. Originally, the cards were without any printing. How would you know the front from the back and the top from the bottom? Problem solved.

Spinning Things

That television pitcure of cards being swallowed up by a machine was fine but the preferred camera shot was always the spinning reels on a tape drive. If you were an audiophile back then, you knew instinctively that computer tape drives were just overgrown audio tape recorders. They were bigger, but they worked just like the open reel audio tape recorders in use at the time. For the rest of the viewing audience, they were just spinning wheels. The tape itself was usually too thin and moved too fast to really be seen on TV. But the motion was impressive anyway.

Fact is, computer tapes worked exactly like audio tapes with only one exception - what was recorded on the tape. Rather than recording audio variations, these tape drives recorded the codes that represented data. Numbers and alphabetic characters. The code was somewhat similar to that punched into each column of an IBM card. The tape format provided an extremely compact method of data storage since each tape could hold the information from thousands of punched cards. Tape media provided both temporary storage of data while the computer was manipulating information and permanent storage for the end results.

Perhaps you have seen video of tape drives that included the lower section of the machine. There, below the spinning reels you undoubtedly noticed 2 vertical metal columns with loops of tape that danced along as the reels moved. The columns existed to cushion the tape during rapid starts and stops. The loops prevented stretching the tape. That loop of tape in the column was held there by vacuum and the reel motors were actually controlled by sensors in the columns. They worked independently of the sudden movements at the read/write head where the data was actually recorded or read back.

729 Tape Drives for 1400 Series Computers

Soon enough the spinning wheels evolved into spinning platters or disks as the technological advances continued. The first data disks were 24" in diameter and could hold a whopping 100,000 "bytes" or characters each. The disk itself was a very smooth metal platter that was coated with a layer of magnetic material. Originally that material was iron oxide just like an audio tape or cassette. Yes, rust can be useful, even in a computing system! Eventually the disks shrunk and smoother magnetic materials were found. Current disk surfaces are shiny like chrome, come as small as 1" in diameter and some might contain a terabyte or more of data. By the way, a terabyte is equal to a million million bytes or characters. Unfortunately for the TV people, once again there was not much to see. But all was good. By then viewers were more familiar with computers thanks to games.

Go Play

Strange as it may sound, games were an important part of computer history. People have always had a natural fear of the unknown. Think about it. How close would you stand to an intercontinental missile? How close to a nuclear reactor? People who understand those things respect them but do not fear them.

Computers were the same. There was something super-cerebral about computers. Computers are for those egg-heads at MIT. Don't get too close. You might break something. Those in the computer industry knew what was coming. They knew that eventually all of us would be using computers. Problem. How do you overcome that fear?

The solution to overcoming that fear was to let people play with the computers. First there were very simplistic games like ping-pong. Then the games became more sophisticated like maybe Tetris. Add thought to the game such as in Dungeons and Dragons. Kids today have no fear mostly because of games.

Some of us still may have problems with the "damn computer" that changed the screen "all by itself." But few truly fear the computer. Take a break. Go play games for a while.

Evolving terminology

With technological change came new words and changes in terminology. Even so, some terms remained the same. At one time, a computer operator "loaded" a program into a computer from a "deck of cards."   The operator "mounted" a reel of tape on the tape drive. Operators still say they "load" a program despite the card decks being long gone. Tapes and interchangeable disk packs may be gone in favor of permanent hard drives, but disks are still "mounted" to inform the program that all is ready to proceed.

Another fun term that may be physically obsolete but has endured in the industry over the years is "bit bucket." This term was used to describe the destination of data when a machine malfunctioned. As in "Everything was fine until that CPU error dumped everything in the bit bucket." The term originated with the machines that punched the codes into IBM cards. The keypunch machines. When holes were punched in a card, the bits (tiny rectangular card chips) were funneled to and stored in a small container called a chip box or bit bucket. Occasionally the operator was required to empty it like a waste basket.   The term also became the punch line for inside jokes. "Problem? What problem? It was just a full bit bucket."

The businesses themselves changed over the years too. Early tabulating machines became "data processing machines" before they were obsoleted by computing systems. At one time, computer "jobs" were scheduled to run sequentially.   Now many computer jobs (programs) can be run at the same time thanks to "operating system software" which can do juggling acts through "multi-programming" and "virtual memory." Those terms are complicated enough that we'll just call it software magic for the moment. Later we'll look at more detail.

* * * * *

An interesting side note. In earlier times you could easily tell those people who worked with computers. Invariably they were the ones with IBM cards protruding from behind the pens and pencils in their shirt pocket "nerd packs." An unpunched IBM card was perfect for making notes. It was stiff enough to write on while holding it in the palm of your hand and the perfect size for shirt pockets.

2 -The Repairman

The Field Engineer/Customer Engineer job underwent significant changes over time, but its basis remained firmly planted in the past. A short history illustrates how the job retained all the original elements while evolving with the technology.

The repairman cometh

In the early days of the C-T-R Corporation, when one of Herman Hollerith's machines broke down, he would send out one of his engineers to fix the problem. Once at the customer site, the engineer would analyze the problem, obtain whatever parts were necessary and make the repair. Afterwards he would document the failure as to its cause and what was necessary to return the machine to functionality. He took this information back to the factory for analysis and possible future improvements. If the same part wore out or broke multiple times, there was need for improvement. It was sort of a re-engineering process. At that time, tabulating machines were mostly rented from the manufacturer rather than purchased. They were simply too expensive for most companies to buy outright. Therefore, the manufacturer treated its machines as assets. It was very important to keep the machines in operation and improvements were always beneficial.

As the tabulating business grew, it became apparent that Hollerith was in need of more engineers just to maintain the machines he had leased or sold. He simply could not afford to have his design and manufacturing engineers scattered about the country. He needed them to be designing newer and better machines. So, he hired engineers just to keep his machines running.

Since these new people would be working out in the field at various customer locations rather at the main office, he named them Field Engineers. Furthermore, because of the mechanical nature of tabulating machines, these Field Engineers needed to be primarily Mechanical Engineers but with some electrical knowledge as well. By the beginning of the Mainframe Era, there were literally tens of thousands of these Field Engineers around the world repairing hundreds of thousands of "card-based" machines.

14

Old gray iron

The old tabulating machines were sturdily built, heavy, mechanical machines. That meant hundreds of moving parts that required adjustment, maintenance and regular lubrication. At the same time, the mechanical mechanisms were electrically controlled by switches, solenoids and relays. Those mechanisms needed to be clean and free of oil and greases. Obviously that was one source of problems.

As the business expanded and matured into data processing and computers, the tabulating machines became known as the "old gray iron." The name originated with Hollerith's choice of paint color – a dark gray. The color was chosen to help hide dirt and smudges from lubricating oils or grease. Spanning the two disciplines of mechanics and electricity made for many unique situations. Field Engineers required training in mechanics and electrical circuits... and how to keep them separated.

In late in 1959, IBM announced the first widely available commercial computer, the IBM 1400 System. It was not an instant replacement for those tabulating machines. Yet keeping up with the demand for this all new type of business machine was a problem. Demand was such that a customer often waited a year or even two years for delivery of his first computer. In the meantime, that old gray iron kept the business going. Even when the computer finally arrived, it still took months to write and test the programs that allowed the computer to replace the "tab" machines. The "computer revolution" actually took many years rather than months. While this was transpiring, the Field Engineer had to add a third discipline to his knowledge. Electronics.

The need for many

The advent of transistors transformed computers. That, in turn, changed the Field Engineering job. Even though the majority of problems would still be mechanical in nature, the FE needed even broader knowledge of electronic circuitry. Computer equipment manufacturers now needed Electronics Engineers who were also Mechanical Engineers. As time went on and technology evolved, Field Engineering people would become more specialized. Soon, some FEs were trained to work exclusively on computers. Remember that the majority of the equipment was still mechanical in nature, so those skill requirements remained.

The blockbuster event of 1964 was IBM's announcement of the System/360. This was a totally new concept in business computers. It was a scalable system. There was a whole family of mainframe computers. There were models suitable for small businesses and others large enough to run international corporations, research projects and for government use. The word at the time was that IBM CEO Thomas J. Watson Jr. "bet the company" on this new product line. He put the company deeply in debt with multiple banks and institutions to finance the project. Fortunately for him (and really all of us), his gamble paid off big time.

* * * * *

We humans are taught mathematics in terms of the decimal system. We count to ten using the digits 0 thru 9. In everyday use, we often think of zero as meaning nothing. However mathematicians see it as equally significant with the other digits. When we count more than 10, we use multiples of 10 – tens, hundreds, thousands, etc.

Computers are based on simple switches that are either on or off. So internally, the computer uses the simple binary system utilizing only the digits 0 and 1. Naturally, you can't get very far on one and none, so computers use groups of those digits to represent data. Instead of multiples of ten, as we do, computers use multiples of 2 – twos, fours, eights, and so on. Earlier computer systems had used groups of three zeroes and ones ("bits") to enable them to count 0 thru 7. So 3 "bits" made one octal digit. A pair of octal digits (a total of 6 bits) were required to represent a character. Together, the two octal digits could represent 64 different characters.

The new System/360 architecture was totally new. The new system upped the game by adding one more "bit" to each 'digit' so the computer could now count to 16 rather than just 8. This was the first commercially available "hexadecimal" computer. It still took two of these digits to represent a character, but now the combination could represent 256 different characters. Changing the basic mathematics made the system four times as powerful as its forbearers. All of today's computers continue to use this hexadecimal or "hex" mathematics.

16

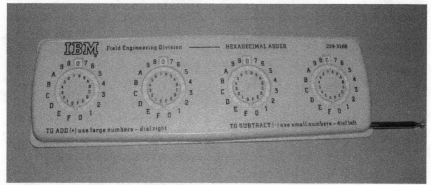

An aid used to make adding and subtraction easier for humans who were only taught the decimal system.

Utilizing this new common architecture meant that a program written to run for one mainframe could be run on any of the other models. There was also one common set of peripheral devices – the input and output machines that could be connected to any model mainframe. For the record, Input and Output were almost always shortened to the simple term "I/O."

Of course the massive shift to a new architecture necessitated all Field Engineers be retrained. And lest we forget, all the mechanical aspects of a computing system remained.

Just as in Herman Hollerith's day, once again recruitment of more Field Engineers was underway. The company needed hundreds of new Field Engineers who were knowledgeable in both electronics and mechanics. The weeding out of applicants meant testing in all the aspects of all disciplines as well as communications skills to deal with customers. Recruitment became a long process.

3. From whence they came

Often posed is the question: "Does the man fit the job or does the job fit the man?" In the Field Engineering world, the answer is the former. The computer companies knew what basic characteristics worked best for the FE job. Those characteristics had been well established through years of experience. Although Field Engineers came in every shape, size, gender and color, their core values were pretty much peas in a pod. On the other hand, as we will see these people were definitely not clones. In fact you would hard pressed to identify a Field Engineer on his day off.

What it took

Field Engineers seldom came from rich families. They were not Ivy League School graduates. They came from working class families. Urban neighborhoods. Middle-class suburbia. Rural farm communities. Many had immigrant grandparents and even parents who still spoke their native tongue with only "broken English." Others came from families that still remembered the Great Depression.

Common to all was that their parents were willing to do whatever it took to make a better life for their children. They were hard working families who considered it a major failing to accept charity of any kind. A good work ethic was taught from birth.

Those Mainframe Mechanics born in the 1930's remember the WWII days of rationing and the origin of recycling. They remember saving aluminum foil and balls of string. They remember "recapped" tires on the cars. The author remembers helping weed the Victory Garden and the father who worked in a "defense plant" where the exact product produced was never talked about. Those were character building days of "making do" and fixing things to make them last a little longer.   Field   Engineers   were   do-it-yourselfers.

Overall, few FEs were able to afford 4-year degrees. However, their parents ensured they were high school graduates. Many did have some college level courses under their belts. Community Colleges did not exist yet, but many worked their way through technical schools. A Certificate was what could be afforded at the time. Also, most being veterans, they availed themselves of the GI Bill to take college night classes or mail-order courses of all kinds.

Military

Most Field Engineers were veterans. Some of the old-timers had served in the Korean War and many were stationed there in the years that followed. Many served in Vietnam. Back then all young men were subject to the draft. When your number came up and you received greetings from Uncle Sam, you were off to spend a couple years defending your country.

Boot camp was a never a favorite part of the military, yet the old Mainframe Mechanics will tell you that in the end, they appreciated it and were glad to have had the experience. It was the place everyone worked hard, grew strong mentally as well as physically and learned discipline... or else. It created mature men out of boys. That maturity was important to corporate recruiters.

A funny thing about Field Engineers was that the majority spent more than the required two years in military service. The majority spent time in the Navy or Marines, some in the Air Force and a slight minority were in the Army. There were multiple reasons for that. Of course there were a few that were "gung-ho" and wanted to join for the action. For others it was following the family tradition in one particular branch of the service. But for many, it was about the education.

Being drafted meant going where the military needed you. Tank driver. Artillery crewman. Foot soldier. None of those offered much of a future beyond the military. On the other hand, the Air Force offered airframe or jet engine mechanics training. The Navy offered diesel mechanics, pattern making and eventually nuclear maintenance. The Army offered helicopter, truck and diesel mechanics, etc. But most of all they all offered various electronics training options. These choice jobs had futures beyond the military. The snag was they were only available to those who enlisted. This was not a ploy. It was practical. These jobs required much more training. Even for the government, it did not make much sense to spend most of a year training someone who would only be there for one more year.

Different but the same

Barring the job requirement similarities, everyone's background was unique. Perhaps the easiest way to illustrate that is through a few examples.

There was one fellow who was originally from Quebec, where his father owned a gas station. Harry and his older brother grew up working at the station. They worked long hours, 6 days a week. He was thankful that they lived in the French speaking province because everything closed on Sunday. That gave him a break from the boring family business. He knew there was no way to afford the college education necessary for a better life.

Harry left his family and immigrated to Connecticut. Once here, he joined the US Air Force. He knew that our Air Force offered excellent training in electronics. He had heard that USAF training was far superior to that available in Canada. Best of all the US offered citizenship to those who completed a "hitch" in the military. It was the perfect alternative to a boring life. Near the end of his enlistment, Harry heard of the opportunities in Field Engineering.

Another example was Ray. He was from a small farming town in Pennsylvania. He worked hard, saved his money and obtained a certificate from a technical school in Pittsburgh. The school helped him find a job as a Field Engineer. The down side was that it required his moving to another city. Then, not long after completing his initial company training, he was drafted into the Army. Fortunately the Army needed some electronics repairmen and his education and new job fit perfectly. Following boot camp and military electronics training he was assigned to a repair depot stateside. After his stint in the Army, Ray returned to his waiting Field Engineering job.

The last example is a suburban kid who had tinkered with radios and TVs since before high school but not having particularly impressive grades or rich parents, he never could afford a formal education. After bouncing around a few years with low paying insecure jobs, he realized his life was going nowhere. He decided to join the Army to get the formal electronics training necessary for a real job.

It turned out that he did well in the Army school and he was asked to remain as an instructor in the course he had joined to learn. During off duty hours, he also studied on his own and eventually passed the tests for a First Class FCC License. That assured him a job in the radio and TV broadcast industry after the military.

Upon discharge, he worked briefly at that career until a better opportunity came along. The rapidly growing computer industry was in need of Field Engineers. The promise of better pay and more stability could not be ignored.

That is a small sampling of the diverse backgrounds of Field Engineers. These guys also came from ghettos, barrios and even included a few college grads. The common denominators were not so much high intelligence or outgoing personalities. The job required self-starting individuals with maturity and especially a willingness and ability to learn. With technology changing constantly, there would always be new things to learn.

Getting Hired

Nowadays, the hiring process starts with an unknown individual reading an online resume and sight unseen, deciding who gets an interview with an "HR Specialist." Back in the mainframe era the process was far different. It involved real testing and real interviews with the management a person would be working for.

Testing was often an all day affair of timed tests for spatial ability, logical thinking, mathematical skills, decision making, and psychological disposition. Those passing the tests were generally subjected to at least two interviews. One interview would be with the manager for whom the applicant would be working. The discussion usually addressed the resume and work experiences. Another would be with a second level manager where personality was evaluated. Occasionally a third interview with another first level manager was sandwiched between the two.

With the applicants resume and test results in hand, the interviewers would then discuss the applicant and decide whether or not to hire. Hiring decisions were generally made within the week. New hires often started work the following Monday.

The First of Many Schools

The first day on the job as a Field Engineer was filled with introductions and making plans for attending the three month long Basic Training School. Most often the trainee attended this school in Endicott, NY where IBM's first factory was located. The alternative was Rochester, MN. Not the best place during the winter months.

Field Engineering Basic Training was actually the beginning a career long education process. It consisted of a series of courses beginning with entry level machines and progressing to the newer, more complicated ones. This Basic Training school originated in 1928 and the beginning portions had changed little over the decades. The trainee was always aware that he was one step from the door until he finished the entire series of courses.

Everyone was first trained on the maintenance, repair and troubleshooting of "unit record" machines. The unit record referred to machines that handled punched cards, which IBM for obvious reasons, called IBM cards. These basic machines included the keypunch where data was punched into the cards and the sorters which did just that. Few trainees had any prior experience with this equipment. These were all specialized machines for what was then called "data processing." Keypunches and card sorters existed in no other industry.

Trainees with previous electronics experience often confronted an immediate problem. They were familiar with electronic diagrams, the schematics that represented the electrical connections within the equipment.   However, keypunch diagrams were not electronic diagrams.   These machines predated the now familiar electronic diagrams.   These schematics were drawn using symbols from the telephone and telegraph industry. Immediately trainees were forced to learn a new language.

An IBM 026 keypunch machine.   Courtesy Flicker photo sharing.

Moving Right Along

Following the introduction of computers, Field Engineering was split into two groups; those who worked on the traditional machines and those who were dedicated to computing equipment. The more complicated unit record machines included calculators, collators, interpreters and, of course, tabulators. The FEs in the computer group were trained on the "I/O" or input and output machines attached to mainframe computers. Initially those included card readers and punches, printers and the tape drives that were used for data storage.

We will see these machines in more detail later. For now it is important to note these computer machines were still mostly mechanical in nature. All those moving parts needed lubrication and adjustment and were subject to the same frailties as the unit record machines. Electronics was added to allow the machines to communicate or interface with the computer itself.

Notably absent from this training was the disk drive. Disk drives were a technological breakthrough that for the first time allowed random access to data. The previous storage device, the tape drive, allowed only sequential access. The earliest disk drives were huge, expensive and delicate machines. It wasn't until 1961 that smaller,

23

more practical machines were introduced. Accordingly, throughout the 1960s disk drives were considered advanced machines and were taught separately.

The IBM 305 RAMAC, the first "hard drive"

Likewise, the computer mainframe was an advanced course. With a range of mainframe sizes and models, each was taught individually in detail.

Graduation

Having survived Basic Training, trainees were traditionally treated to a formal graduation ceremony and dinner. The dinner came complete with congratulatory speeches by staff and a guest speaker. The speaker at the author's graduation dinner was the IBM Vice-President of Research. I still marvel at the glimpse of the future he gave us back in 1966.

Among a wide variety of topics, he spoke of tiny fiberglass strands that would replace copper wires. He explained how copper wires slowed everything down because they had resistance. The fiber optics had no resistance. He said even telephone wires would give way to these strands of fiberglass. He also warned this would create "the last mile problem." That was the cost of changing the wires leading from telephone poles to every house in the country. But then he said not to worry. By then everybody would probably carry their own personal telephone wherever they went.

He spoke of how, someday, lasers would proliferate and be used to transfer data and even print data on paper. Lasers would also be able to print data on plastic disks. He saw technological advances that would shrink big mainframe computers to a size able to fit in a briefcase.

The last thing he said was, "The career you embark on is a very new type of career. It did not exist just a few years ago. During your careers, the only constant will be change. And in all likelihood, your job will disappear before you retire." The accuracy of those words was amazing.

Changes were in progress even as this Field Engineer was just getting his feet wet. We were working for the Field Engineering Division, but we were no longer Field Engineers. As mentioned at the beginning, the job title had just been changed to Customer Engineer. Our customers really did identified with us and often asked us for advice or opinion on pending decisions and purchases. Occasionally we would be taken aside and asked if something the salesman said was really true or just sales bullshit.

During that 32+ year career, there was an ever evolving job, multiple job title changes, a couple division changes and six different company CEOs. No matter what they chose to call us, we would always be Customer Engineers to our customers.

From here, where?

Many words have been used just to put a background in place. But this was who we were and where we came from. Customer Engineer was a job that was respected (mostly) and even prestigious to some (but not us). At the same time, it was often dirty, backbreaking, and disruptive to family life. It was even loathed by some customer management, especially those discovering their system was "STILL down." It was definitely not a boring 9 to 5 job.

Obviously electronic circuits did not have moving parts, so they simply did not fail very often. The majority of our labors were elsewhere in the mechanical and other aspects of a computing system. CEs handled everything – electronic, mechanical, operational, program code and occasionally people.

By nature, CEs prefer to remember the brighter side of those days. That is not to say tales of coming home filthy dirty or dog tired from an "all-nighter" or of getting into trouble with customers have been excluded here. Remember, we CEs often referred to ourselves as mainframe mechanics. White shirts or not, there was much hard, dirty work involved too.

There was once a cartoon that depicted a two-story office building with windows open wide and people throwing flowers down on a man walking toward the entrance. The man carried a briefcase that was labeled Computer Repairman. Believe me that never happened in real life.

Oh yes, a warning. For clarity, names are used throughout this book. First names only... which may or may not correspond to real people. One thing can be assured - if you read it here, it happened. You need only ask an old CE if things like this really occurred. The answer will come with a quick nod and, "oohh yeah." Then be prepared for his experience stories.

4 - Corporate culture

Until recent times, IBM Corporation was mainly a manufacturer of machines, so sales drove the company. Those in the sales division considered themselves the elite. After all, "nothing happens until you sell something." Sales offices were divided mostly by geography, but there were also separate offices for such things as computer supplies and software sales. Manufacturing facilities were separated along product lines. In other words, they were just like any other large manufacturing company.

The Field Engineering Division was different. Field Engineering did not make anything and it did not sell any products. Since the computer systems needed to be installed and maintained, the Field Engineering Division was often considered a necessary evil. The stepchild so to speak. But that distinction was cherished by those of us who worked there. The FE Division was clearly different. Customer Engineers considered themselves the good guys. CEs not only installed and maintained the equipment, they were also the ones who straightened out the problems caused by others.

* * * * *

Remember Business 101 class? The Theory X, Theory Y thing? To refresh your memory, Theory X basically says all employees are lazy so you must keep after them constantly to keep them productive. Threaten to fire them if they do not work fast enough or hard enough. Theory Y says employees actually want to do their jobs. Tell them what needs done and leave them alone. All they need is a little guidance and an occasional pat on the back. Field Engineering Division, more so than any other division, followed Theory Y.

The laid-back culture in Field Engineering was even necessary. True, FE Division included the usual office staff, personnel department and accounting people. But the "troops", the Customer Engineers, were scattered all over at customer locations. CEs were assigned to customer accounts based on their training and the size of the customer. In some cases, multiple CEs were assigned to a single large customer account.

27

One huge customer was Boeing Corporation. In fact Boeing was so large, an entire FE branch office resided at Boeing's Seattle complex. At the other end of the spectrum, one CE might be assigned multiple small customer accounts. Obviously management could not hover. CEs had to be self-starters.

Principles and Traditions

From the time of T. J. Watson Sr., the IBM Corporation was a company of principles and tradition. Watson had defined 3 basic principles: 1) Respect for the individual, 2) The best customer service and 3) Superior accomplishment of all tasks. Those principles made it a great company and a great company to work for. Through good times and bad, there had never been a layoff. Not even during the Great Depression.

To encourage a "think before you act" culture, the famous Think sign was everywhere. The signs were on almost every desk. Thousands of these simple signs were given away to customers as well.

One of the early Think signs.

Dress Code

Although it was officially denied, there really was a dress code. Just that was not written down. It had been handed down by word of mouth for decades. Rumor was the original CEO, Tom Watson Sr. had personally started it by saying that he thought company people should dress in such a manner as to be indistinguishable from their customers. At the time, a suit, long sleeved white shirt and conservative tie was the choice of executives, salesmen and customer management. This informal code was "encouraged" through casual comments by managers to their subordinates. "Isn't that orange tie a bit robust?"

To the CE working on his equipment, such a dress code could be a problem. The expected "uniform" did not work well when replacing a heavy power supply or rebuilding the hydraulic unit of a 1403 line printer. The suit and tie were still expected. However, the way engineers think, there is always another, better way. Consequently the standard CE uniform became a short-sleeved white shirt and the suit coat always came off at the door. Also CEs always bought suits that came with 2 pairs of pants.

* * * * *

In the early 70s, light blue shirts became a business fashion rage. It was a strange fad because the craze had been initiated years before by television people. Back in the days of black and white television, the stark white shirts caused a technical problem called blooming on the black and white TV screens. It was due to the high contrast with darker suits and ties. Therefore light blue shirts were worn by announcers and actors. They still looked white on TV. Anyway, customers and CEs picked up on that trend. Management tolerated it because of the many customers who had also followed the trend.

Naturally, fashion cannot stand still. Sales depend on new trends. Soon dress shirts appeared in all sorts of pastel shades. Then the shirts became bolder in color. It is obvious were this is heading. Most CEs reserved white shirts for big meetings, trips to the office or if they ran out of blue, green, yellow, gray, pink, etc.

* * * * *

29

About that time, our local office was run by a very conservative "bean counter" type Branch Manager. One January morning, I had been helping out at our Data Center which was located in the same building as our branch office. Yep, I wore the gold shirt (do you remember 70s gold?) my wife gave me that Christmas. The inevitable happened as we headed to the basement cafeteria for a cup of coffee. I passed our Branch Manager in the elevator lobby. With no particular emotion, he said, "That's a rather dark shirt isn't it?" I replied, "My wife got it for me. She thought it was right in style." Probably not the best thing to say.

Later that day, I had occasion to go upstairs to our office. My manager spotted me and asked me to step in for a moment. He had obviously been informed of my short conversation with the guy in the "corner pocket." For those who don't know, the big boss always got the corner office because it had windows on two sides, not just one. Of course the subject of shirts was brought up.

Also at the time, I was assigned three separate customer accounts, all within less than a mile of each other. They were also totally different types. There was a small insurance company, a manufacturer of heavy industrial equipment and an urban college. I won't name the insurance company because it is now a huge national corporation with an even larger advertising budget. The equipment manufacturer has since gone out of business. The college grew to become Cleveland State University.

At any rate, my manager set out to explain that fashion trends were not always in line with our business interests. I thought about that for a minute, considering my situation. Then I interrupted his speech, "You know, you're right. A white shirt and a gray suit would be appropriate at *the insurance company* and I can always wear coveralls when I go to *the heavy equipment manufacturer*, but I can't grow a beard that fast for CSU... and I won't wear flip-flops anywhere." Never heard another word about my shirts.

* * * * *

Even with colored shirts, the suit and tie were still an issue for CEs. There was not much we could do about the suits or shirts, but ties

30

were another matter. Many CEs expressed their individualism through their ties.

As it happened, I married a gal who, in addition to her other talents, was a seamstress who could adroitly remake her clothes to fit properly and hem skirts and pants in a flash. Occasionally, she made me a tie as a birthday or Christmas gift. She did a great job so I did not mind getting that Father's Day tie. There was one complaint she always expressed. It was very difficult to find material suitable for making ties. The available materials were generally too soft, so they required the addition of a stiffening material to make them lay smooth and flat. Hold that thought a moment.

Our living room was sorely in need of a new sofa. The wife and I visited several furniture stores before finding the perfect replacement sofa. We chose the style and were trying to find an appropriate upholstery fabric. Suddenly she said, "That's it!" I asked if that was the sofa fabric she liked. She said, "No. No. The fabric! It's perfect for ties." From that point on, I had a huge selection of ties. A few of those ties have survived the decades and my sons' pilfering.

Have you ever considered how wild some upholstery fabrics can be?

Quarter Century Club

At most companies employees must wait until retirement before getting recognition for their years of service. You know, the usual retirement party. The office gang. Some food, refreshments and the retirement gift. However, in a tradition going back to the 1920s, IBM recognized employees after twenty-five years of service. The milestone was recognized with a dinner and a gift of the employee's choice. Just before reaching the twenty-five year mark, the employee was given a catalog illustrating many high quality gifts from which to choose. Selections were made in time to have the gift engraved before a formal presentation on the anniversary. My choice was a Rolex wristwatch. It is still the most expensive jewelry I own. From then on, the employee was a member of the Quarter Century Club.

As a member, the employee was invited to attend the annual club dinner. The dinners were annual until the size of the company and the number of people who stayed with IBM their whole career overwhelmed it. The dinners continued but bi-annually. The best part was that when you retired, you still had a retirement party!

Open doors

Another tradition, based on the first IBM principle (Respect for the individual), was the "open door" policy. At any time, any employee could walk into any manager's office to discuss a problem. Business or personal, it did not matter. Generally this meant talking to your immediate manager, but you could go over his head at any time. Exercising that privilege was more common than one might think.

I availed myself of the open door only once. It involved our internal company mail. Each of us had a mailbox in the office. We could stop in any time and pick up our mail. Once a week, our secretary would gather any remaining mail and send it to our homes. In the early 1990s, when the business climate changed, somewhere far above our office level, someone decided to save money by doing away with the office mailrooms. The job was outsourced. Staff was replaced by a contracted third party. The mailroom staff did not lose their jobs. They transferred to other jobs or were retained by the new contractor. We were assured that the third-party company was fully bonded and the change would be transparent.

Shortly after the change took place, my weekly home mailing included an envelope that was boldly marked "Personal and Confidential." It had been slit open. The envelope contained a complete copy of my personnel records, my training list and included compensation information. It was intended for me to verify or update as necessary. The next day I headed to the "corner pocket" to talk to our Branch Manager.

The Branch Manager agreed with the severity of the intrusion and immediately phoned the Area Manager. Area also agreed and promised to follow up. A week later, I got a message to stop by at my convenience. The Branch Manager began by apologizing. Obviously not a good sign. He explained that he and the Area Manager escalated the situation to the division level where they also received apologies but were told nothing further would be done. The corporate decision was that the contract was in place and they were sure my personal information had not been compromised. We did not realize it at the time, but that was a preliminary indication of corporate wide changes to come. The new way of doing business in America.

The survey

With most of us scattered about, it was difficult for the company to gauge employee morale, etc. The solution was an annual anonymous survey. It was carefully crafted by psychologists and covered everything from our impression of what customers thought of the company to our personal opinion of management teams to how we thought our company was fairing in the stock market. Each question included room for write-in comments as well.

About a month after a survey was completed, the office received a detailed report of the results, including an anonymous list of comments. Managers would huddle and discuss the results and how they might address any areas that needed attention. Then a territory meeting was held to discuss the results with the CEs. Believe it or not, it was mostly a very adult give and take session. A true discussion. Everyone appreciated the cantor. And we all loved to read the comments.

Executive interview

The company had many people oriented traditions and a few requirements. Every employee was required to meet with his second level manager once a year for the annual Executive Interview. Normally this meant the boss asking how things were going, if the employee had any concerns about his immediate manager and if the employee had any suggestions for improvements in the office. It was his chance to get a feel for office morale, etc. Again, these were generally relaxed encounters.

* * * * *

Remember that bean counter Branch Manager? In a way it was sad. He was just not a people person. He truly was consumed by numbers and ran the office based on reports. He reminded me of some politicians who made their decisions based on the polls. An executive interview with him was different. He would open a binder to find the latest reports dealing with your territory and personal performance. His only interest was keeping the numbers at the correct level.

That annual survey I mentioned before? The first survey after his arrival was a disaster. The follow up meetings were all about the numbers. We never did find out the results of the second annual survey under his management. Rather than the usual territory gatherings to discuss the results, he called for an all-hands office meeting. When it was his turn at the lectern, he began with, "I just don't understand it. We met all our goals this year, and yet you people are still unhappy. We need a more professional attitude here." There was absolute silence. Nobody remembers what was said after that. A few months later, he was promoted to a different part of the country. I often wonder if he ever "got it."

The Club

Another way our company took care of its employees was the IBM Club. It was basically a social club for all employees. Each location had its own locally run Club. The only corporate involvement was money donated to each location based on head count. This donation was designated for two annual events – a Family Picnic and a Christmas party for the kids. All planning and execution was at the local level by elected employees and volunteers. Management participation was limited to an advisory role. Most often, the summer picnics would alternate between a reasonably close theme park and a good old fashioned picnic outing with games for all. The Christmas party always gave gifts to every child 12 and under. There was entertainment and naturally, Santa and his elves helped distribute the gifts.

Other social events were encouraged with event fees covering the costs. With all volunteer help, fees were minimal. There were dozens of different events throughout the year to satisfy most every taste. And I mean everything. There were round and square dances, clam bakes, steak roasts, automobile rallies, excursions, softball games, bowling leagues, etc. Square dances in particular were always fun as they included lessons. Who could remember all those steps from one time to the next?

Activities also included charitable work. Our location took under its wing Camp Cheerful, a camping experience exclusively for handicapped children. Children were afforded weeklong stays in a secluded, heavily wooded park setting. They had cabins, sporting fields and a large central hall that was used for dining, parties, etc. Our volunteers would coordinate weekend work parties to clean up, fix up and paint up as necessary. As reward, we were allowed to use the hall a couple times a year for our events. Everyone benefited.

This was long before the emergence of Silicon Valley companies and their unusual employee-friendly perks. With that sort of corporate culture, the majority of employees spent their entire careers in one place. The company benefited too. The internal culture extended itself through employee to customer relationships.

Through the early 60s, few customers utilized their computers more than during normal business hours. They simply did not have enough work to keep the machines busy during the off hours. And computers were not only expensive to buy, they were expensive to operate.

As more computer applications appeared companies began to realize the efficiency of 24/7 operation. Some, whose own work was limited, began selling their 'extra time' to others not so fortunate as to own a computer. This practice became known as time-sharing. And as time went on, enterprising individuals created companies solely for the purpose of time-sharing. They were often called "service bureaus."

As more and more applications were computerized, the amount of surplus time was reduced. Other companies were buying their own systems as computer prices came down. Soon time-sharing gave way to in-house round the clock operations.

Shift Work

As expected, the Field Engineering workload became a multi-shift operation as well. In our office we eventually had four to five CEs covering 2nd shift on a permanent basis. Two more CEs covered the grave yard shift.

When one of the regular 2nd shift CEs was attending an extended school, I became his replacement. The workload at night was spotty and generally light since it dealt only with malfunctioning machines. For the most part there was no preventative maintenance to be performed and installations or meetings were unheard of. This resulted in night shift CEs often meeting at a convenient restaurant for dinner.

One summer evening four of us happen to have been near the downtown area. One CE remembered seeing an all-night diner, so we decided to meet there for dinner. There were only three or four customers at the large counter and a few more at a couple tables as we walked in. Within five minutes, they were all gone. We had the place to ourselves. One CE finally said, "I think the other customers thought we were police detectives." We had a good laugh when we realized what those customers had just witnessed: Here it was a warm summer evening. Four guys walk in wearing suits. Each has a bulge on his hip under the jacket (the pagers). There are three white guys and one black guy.

Obstacles

There were a few obstacles to overcome when working other than normal business hours. A closed main office was the most obvious. This usually meant entering the customer location through some alternate guarded entrance and a long walk back to the computer room. In some cases it meant a golf cart ride through the factory to the office back door. Every company was different. None used the front door.

Woody was one of the regular graveyard shift CEs. He knew all the customer nighttime routines well. On one occasion, an in-town manufacturing company required service on a tape drive. The computer room was on the 2nd floor in the middle of its rather long headquarters building.

During normal business hours this was never a problem. The CE simply walked in the main lobby entrance and signed in. The receptionist would buzz him into the main hallway. Not far to the right of the lobby door was a stairway that emerged directly across from the computer room door. Off-hours presented the challenge. It was necessary to call ahead for a guard to come and unlock the chained main entrance doors and then buzz the CE into the hallway. Exiting involved the reverse procedure.

After completing the call at this account, Woody called the guard to meet him down in the lobby to let him out. He then made another quick call to his next customer to let them know he was on his way. Woody then exited to the lobby. The guard was not there yet. He waited about ten minutes, then using the receptionist's phone, called the guard shack. They said a guard was on his way.

Once in the lobby, he was trapped. To get back in required the buzzer at the receptionist's desk. Too far from the door. The two outside doors, equipped with push bars for exit, were chained together to prevent being opened from the inside. Another 10 minutes went by. Woody knew his next customer would be awaiting his arrival. Again he called explaining to the guard that he had now been waiting close to half an hour. He was told to be patient. The guard laughed saying everybody is in a hurry. That was not a good response. Woody told the guard that if no one showed up in another five minutes, he would break out.

Time was up. Still no guard. Woody opened his tool case and pulled out the mini-hacksaw we all carried. The chain was hardened steel so it took a while but the guard never showed. Problem solved. On to his next call.

Eventually the guard found the now unsecured door. We know that because the next day, all hell broke loose. The customer threatened to cancel their contract and remove all our equipment. They wanted that guy fired now! In the end, a new piece of chain resolved the issue.

Callouts

On some occasions, actually more than we care to remember, there were more machine problems than there were CEs working at night or on weekends. There were also times when a rare machine had trouble and only a few CEs were trained to maintain them. At such times, the dispatcher would most likely call the CE responsible for that account. If he was not available, the training lists would be consulted to find an alternate. And that resulted in the dreaded "callout" from home. At whatever time.

A CE might also be called out to assist another CE who found difficulty diagnosing or repairing a problem. Again, the account CE was chosen first since he was most familiar with the account and was better prepared to speak to an irate customer. Naturally, the larger the customer, the greater was the workload for the assigned CE.

Over the years, my wife (and most CE wives) came to hate the telephone. Wives were known to turn off the ringers at night. Some CEs were even known to have installed ringer disconnect switches on telephones not so equipped. Occasionally the phone rang within minutes of crawling into bed. At other times a 3AM call meant not returning home until suppertime that evening. Running all day on a couple hours sleep could take its toll, but that was part of the job.

Official business

One July 4th standby duty was assigned. A call came in for a computer terminal at the Cleveland Police Central Station. The building was located on the near east side of town. On arrival, there were no parking spaces within a several block radius. It strange for a holiday morning downtown, but it was true none the less. After a couple laps, I decided to park directly in front of the police station in an area clearly marked No Parking. I figured this was a holiday and it was official business.

Just past the entrance was a sign-in desk manned by a young (probably a rookie) officer. As I showed my ID and signed the book, he asked where I had parked. Sheepishly I responded, "Out front." "In the no parking zone?" he asked. I said yes, and began explaining about the lack of available parking spaces. With a smile, he said, "Good. You'll be safe there. If you park behind the station or down the street, your car will probably get broken into or stolen." So, OK then!

The problem was a terminal inside the dispatch room. This was before 9-1-1 was invented. Overhearing the dispatchers was distracting to say the least. One caller was complaining about a neighbor illegally shooting off fireworks this early in the day. The dispatcher calmly obtained the address and told the caller they would sent the first available car. Ending the call, he said, "Damn! They think we got a thousand cars just for fireworks!"

Another dispatcher was handling a domestic disturbance call. "Who was it? ... OK, calm down ma'am. You say your husband is drunk? OK. Yes I understand. He's drunk. OK, we'll send someone over. No ma'am. No ma'am, once he sobers up you can't keep him locked out." Lucky for me it was a quick fix and I was on my way home in half an hour.

39

Let him sleep

Another memorable incident involving the Customer Data Center guard comes to mind. With around the clock operation, customers came and went throughout the night. Those customers had to bring their programs and data along as reels of tape and boxes of punched cards. A problem was that the parking lot was located directly behind the building. Customers had to carry their materials around the building and up the front steps. To ease the situation, the guard would often lock up the front and let them enter the rear door where no steps were involved.

On one occasion, a customer was ready to leave. He went to the front reception desk to get the guard so he could unlock the back door. The guard had fallen asleep in his chair. The customer felt sorry for him and decided to let him sleep. Instead, they decided that one of them could crawl out of one of the large awning type windows onto the parking lot. From there the other would pass the tape reels and card boxes to be returned to their office. When done, the second one would crawl out and push the window closed. The guard could enjoy his nap.

All was good until someone in the apartment building across the parking lot spotted two people "stealing stuff" from the building and putting it in their car. He called the police. The guard was startled awake by night sticks pounding on the front door. That one took a while to straighten out, but all ended well... except for the guard, who was never seen again.

Saturday schedule

An increasing workload prompted our office to add a Saturday schedule. Sundays continued to be covered by calling out CEs as needed. We were all asked to take turns covering Saturdays, on a monthly rotation basis. Monday would be the scheduled day off so that we still got two days off in a row. While taking my turn, I decided it was an ideal schedule for me. Our neighborhood was a friendly group of people all about the same age and family size. As a result, Saturdays were often spent talking over the fence rather than doing chores. Sunday was still available for chatting while Monday allowed me to complete my chores while everyone else was at work. Saturday work also meant a little extra money. I worked that schedule for four and a half years until extended schools for new machines and the resulting assignment changes prevented my continuing.

Working Saturday presented some, shall we call them, interesting moments. Our office dispatch room, on the third floor was the usual place to begin the day. The building's first floor was occupied by an IBM Data Center. The Data Center was a place for demonstrations and where customers could schedule time to use an IBM computer for testing or other needs. With other building offices closed on weekends, a guard manned the reception desk at the fishbowl like entrance. To pass the time, the guard often watched a small TV set perched to one side where the cord would reach a receptacle.

Early Saturday was frequently slow so our shift often began with coffee at the next door hotel's coffee shop. On one occasion Don, the other Saturday regular, and I headed over for morning coffee. As we emerged from the elevator and headed toward the front door, Don noticed an old turquoise colored Chevy II parked immediately outside the front door. We recognized it as looking like a car driven by a fellow CE named Tommy and wondered if it was really his.

After coffee, we headed back to the office. I was first to notice the car out front was now gone. As we opened the entrance door, we were discussing the car and why Tommy would have been in the office on a Saturday. The guard glanced up at us, but then shot to his feet and yelled, "My God! My car's gone!" It wasn't Tommy's car after all. Someone managed to break into and drive it off while the guard sat in full view of the street. I guess he was a little too engrossed in watching a TV show. In those days security was more of a running joke than anything about protection.

Herr Boss Man

One Saturday while on that schedule I was called in to relieve a 3rd shift CE who had been working on a nasty control unit problem. The customer was an industrial moving equipment manufacturer. Mostly the company made what is known as tow motors or fork-lifts. Interestingly this company had recently been bought out by a company based in Germany that made similar equipment. The new parent company had sent over a management team for the transition. When I arrived, the computer room supervisor alerted me that the leader of the transition team was on his way in and was very upset due to the extended outage.

Fortunately, we found the intermittent power supply before Herr Boss Man arrived. Unfortunately, our parts room did not normally stock that part. They did, however, locate one at our Chicago parts center. Because of the emergency situation, they were authorized to have it flown in as "next flight out." That meant it would be shipped as baggage on the next available flight. In effect, we were buying a seat for a computer part. This was a very expensive means of obtaining a part, but it was the fastest way and the customer always came first.

For those unfamiliar with German culture, they are generally very formal people who have great respect for authority. I was informed that the transition team manager wished to speak to me. A rather short man in a proper double-breasted suit arrived and stood about 6 feet from me. The computer room supervisor stepped forward and formally introduced him as, "DOCTOR Flöck, the leader of our transition team." With that, the gentleman stepped unusually close with right hand extended, elbow rigidly at his side. He simply said, "I am Flöck." The handshake was one firm pump, no more. My thought, as our eyes met, was the only thing missing was a heel click. I successfully contained my amusement as he took a half-step back.

I explained that we had determined the cause, but the replacement part was not stocked locally due to its size and infrequent use. The replacement power supply was being flown in from Chicago on the next available flight. It would arrive on-site in 6-7 hours. He thought for a moment and then said, "Vun can drrrive to Chicago in four hours, no?" I replied, "Perhaps, but likely a bit more." At that, Dr. Flöck shot back, "Viy do you not rrrent a trrruck?!"

No one had ever heard of GPS or cell phones back then. I think he accepted my explanation that the flight would be faster. After all, that truck driver would first need to get the part, drive city to city, and then navigate unfamiliar streets to find our location.

By this time the regular account CE arrived to babysit the customer until the replacement part arrived. I was able to leave. In the end, we got lucky. Fast work by our Chicago parts center people allowed them to get the part out one flight earlier than expected and our local people were on hand as the plane rolled in. The computer was fully operational a couple hours sooner than expected.

A what?

An embarrassing incident occurred one Easter weekend. Most customers had given their people the weekend off. Don and I sat around the dispatch office all Saturday and we were bored silly. This was way before Google and the internet. Even before Game-Boys. Our stories and those of the dispatcher had run their course.

Finally at mid-afternoon, a call came in. The machine was an "O-10" (actually the machine type was '010'). Neither of us had heard of such a machine. The dispatcher had never heard of it either. Don and I figured that with such a low machine type number that it had to be really old and probably not too difficult to fix. We took the call together just because it was the only call all day.

We were still wondering what sort of machine we had committed to repair as we arrived. The operator, who I knew from previous visits, greeted us saying, "Oh, they sent two of you." We explained how bored we had been and continued to chat for a few minutes. We were leaning back against a row of 4 drawer file cabinets located opposite the computer operator's console. Finally I said, "Well, this is great, but we did come to fix a machine. Where is this '010' you called about?" The operator replied, "Right behind you." I turned around to see a shoebox sized contraption staring back at me. Sure enough, it was labeled "IBM 010."

A relabeled 010 Card Punch. Courtesy pinterest.com.

The machine was an ancient manual card punch that dated back to the 1920s. It consisted of a flat plate on which to place a blank punch card and a series of buttons on top corresponding to the Hollerith code, plus one unmarked button. A card was positioned on the plate at the first column. The appropriate buttons were selected for the desired code to be punched into the first column. Then the unmarked button was pressed to punch the code and advance the card to the second column. The current problem was the advance button did not want to move the card to the next column. The "bug" turned out to be a small piece of torn card wedged where it should not be. We knew it had to be an easy fix. Unfortunately Don often reminded me of the incident with, "Seen any O-10's lately?"

Waterfall

A panic call came in from a downtown savings and loan bank one Saturday afternoon. Their system was "down flat." The operator had pulled the Emergency Power Off switch. They needed a CE to come reset the switch. On arrival, the supervisor escorted me to the third floor and down a hall toward the middle of the building. As we walked, we began to slosh on the carpet. Between the rows of offices on the right was a wide stairway leading up. No longer a stairway, it was a six foot wide waterfall.

The savings and loan headquarters had been built in the mid-nineteenth century atrium or light-shaft style. This style building fills the perimeter of an entire block, but is open in the middle to allow more offices to be exposed to natural light. When the computer age arrived, the S & L could not find a suitable location to house a computer. A computer room required a large open space, additional power, air condition, etc. They decided that rather than buy or build another building somewhere else, they would enclose several floors of the atrium. The addition's first few floors became a parking garage. The third floor afforded a large clear space for a computer room and its associated offices. The new air conditioning equipment was mounted on the roof. It was an interesting solution to the space problem.

In this case, it was not the best solution. On this particular day, a water line had burst in the ceiling of the computer room and it began to literally rain through the tiles of the false ceiling. The operator had managed to pull the Emergency Power Off switch and found some plastic sheeting to cover some of the machines. A janitor shut off the water supply and plumbers had been called. But it was too late.

We cautiously sloshed up the stairs. It was still raining from the ceiling tiles. We returned to his office, which had been spared the flood. He was still very much in panic mode. He had important jobs to be run and wanted to know how long it would take to reset the EPO switch and restore power. I told him, "Not today." He was somewhat relieved to know that our Data Center was available for such emergencies.

Sadly, it took almost a week to repair the pipe and get everything dried out, including under the raised floor. Thanks to it being clean water, the system powered up without any major problems once power was finally restored.

The Customer Engineering job required constant training and updating as new technologies and machines came along. A CE averaged one or three away from home schools a year. The courses of study lasted anywhere from a couple days to several months. Classes for the Central Processing Unit of a mainframe computer generally lasted 2-3 months. And it was not uncommon for a CE to attend 40 to 50 schools over his career.

Interestingly as time went on and the machines became more complicated, the schools got shorter. This was due to the design of the machines and the technology. There were fewer mechanical parts and more diagnostic aids and programs were built into the machines. With these aids, less knowledge of the inner workings of a machine was necessary.

In addition to the formal training, there were dozens and dozens of do-it-yourself courses where CEs learned from books, videos and computer assisted instruction. Following a course, CEs then demonstrated their new-found knowledge via computerized testing. Nowadays, computerized and internet learning are commonplace, but CEs were doing it more than 45 years ago.

Traveling Man

The original Education Centers were located at factory locations. They were in Endicott, Poughkeepsie and Kingston, all in New York state plus one in Rochester, MN to serve the western areas. When a manufacturing facility was built in San Jose, CA another education center was added on the west coast. Later, stand alone Education Centers were added in Chicago, Los Angeles, Washington DC and Atlanta, GA. Over the years, this CE attended multiple classes at all these locations except Rochester, MN. Although stories abounded about Minnesota winters, I was spared that experience.

Transportation to the schools was either by air or car, normally dependent on distance. At each location, lodging was provided at nearby hotels. Customarily two CEs were assigned to a room and those who flew were provided with a rental car when necessary. Although no homework was assigned, CEs sometimes spent evenings going over the materials presented during the class. But generally evenings and weekends were free time. Those within reasonable distances sometimes drove home for the weekend. Others used the time to explore the area and its attractions.

Most schools are vague memories, but a few training experiences do stand out. The first mainframe school I ever attended was the month long System 360 Model 40 class. It is still remembered as the most thorough training ever received. Another school was for the 3800 Printer. This was required to "make it legal" on my training records despite my being "factory trained." (More about that later.) A few others were also memorable.

Charm school

Most of classes were for hardware as some new piece of equipment was introduced. But there were also schools for business practices, procedures, diagnostics, etc. Once there was even something we nicknamed charm school. It was an in-house class at our branch office.

CEs always had a reputation of "calling it like it is" rather than dancing around like some corporate spokesperson explaining a decline in quarterly sales. There was a riddle/story circulating within the company that posed this question: If you saw a group of guys in suits standing in front of the IBM building, how could you tell the Salesmen from the Engineers? The answer was quite simple. You hand each of them a straw hat and a cane. The salesmen would place the hats on their heads at a jaunty angle, twirl the cane and do a dance for you. On the other hand, the CEs would throw the hats on the ground, stomp on them, then beat you over the head with the canes. I will neither confirm nor deny the accuracy of that story.

Apparently the story did have something to do with the required two-day charm school we all attended. The results of that training were inconclusive. We never got any feedback as to its success, but most CEs concluded it was not time well spent.

Oh, You're Here

I once attended a 3-day school for the 7772 Audio Response Unit. Yes, computers could actually talk over 50 years ago! Beginning in January of 1964, IBM had two different Audio Response Units available. Users could make inquiries to a computer via telephone and have this machine respond in English, Spanish or whatever language. Admittedly the vocabulary was limited and the voice was somewhat halting, but in 1964 it was pretty amazing stuff.

Although these machines seemed to run forever, one in my account did break once. I managed to repair it in spite of not being trained, but that is another story. After my assigned machine broke, our management discovered that not one CE in our office was trained on it! The one CE who had been trained had retired a couple years earlier. Not only that, the machine was so rare that classes were very rarely scheduled. The office did summit my name for the next available class which was to be in Poughkeepsie, NY. We simply called that location "Po'ki." Right from the start it was unusual in that I had a hotel room by myself. Logically, I figured I was the lucky odd man in the class.

The next morning, with the class information sheet in hand, I headed to the education building. Once there, I began wandering the halls looking for the assigned room. Most rooms were clearly marked with a number plaque along the edge of the doorframe at eye level. Some of the rooms were not marked. I assumed they were storage rooms or whatever and not classrooms. I did find one unmarked door that was open. I stuck my head into the room to find a class in session. Quickly, I ducked back out. Obviously some of the rooms were missing their ID numbers.

A little farther down the hall, was another open unmarked door. I cautiously stuck my head in to see two guys talking at the far end of the room. One of them looked up and questioned, "John?" Shocked that he knew my name, I responded affirmatively. Then he added, "Great! Now we can get started." This training was so rare that it was a class of only two students. The other CE was local and worked at the factory site. Obviously, they had not scheduled the class until a second student was available.

The instructor pointed out that there would not be the usual hands-on lab portion for the course. They did not have a machine available for our use. Projects such as locating various components had to be done on photos of the machine contained in the course material. We spent most of the time learning the theory of operation and its circuitry. Even the troubleshooting exercises were done in story form with multiple choice answers. It was a bit unnerving to learn a machine without any hands-on time, but what the heck. It never broke.

Protective Gear

IBM had a monster and miracle machine all in one. It was longer than a Cowboy Cadillac and utilized every kind of engineering discipline on the planet. It was not only electronic, but also mechanical, with gears and belts. It utilized air pressure and vacuum. It sported a vibrating platform called a "jogger," to align the documents. In addition, the machine could endorse (stamp) documents, print on them and even photograph each document as it flew by. This machine was the 3890 Document Processor. Although capable of much more, they were used almost exclusively as check sorters. It was capable of processing 2400 checks per minute and then sorting them into as many as 36 different pockets. Like the old IBM Selectric Typewriter before it, it was miraculous that such a contraption could work. But it did.

3890 Document Processor

Near the end of the very long training for this machine was a section on its printer. The printer technology used was an early type of inkjet printing. It had only one ink jet which was controlled electro-statically to print dot matrix characters. Unfortunately printing on checks required a special permanent ink that was known to be a carcinogen. No safer alternative was available. Once the ink dried, there was never a danger to anyone handling the document. The print unit was buried deep inside the machine so operators were never at risk either. But special caution was necessary whenever we worked in the area. To emphasize the safety factors, each student was issued a lab coat, heavy duty green rubber gloves and safety goggles. Some thought it funny and started into the old greeting routine from the M.A.S.H. TV show. Doctor... Doctor... Doctor... Etc.

The next afternoon, we returned to the lab area for some exercises in troubleshooting the print unit. Rob, from Southern California walked in wearing his lab coat, rubber gloves and sunglasses beneath the safety goggles. Above the breast pocket

50

were red magic marker letters spelling "Dr. Strangeglove." We instantly recognized it as a variation on the old Peter Sellers movie, Dr. Strangelove. Before long, everyone sported a doctor nickname. Mine was "Dr. Lefty" which was quite appropriate. Some days were just more fun than others.

Programming too?

Overall, CEs were hardware oriented. Day to day tasks involved electronics and more often mechanical activities. The mainframe mechanics of the 60s and 70s also had more than a passing interest in programming. That was due to the need to understand what was called "machine language." This was the most basic means of communicating with a computer. Every computer program that was ever written had to first be converted into machine language before it was usable. That was done by using another program called a compiler.

The process of creating a computer program has similarities to writing a letter to Auntie Mae. A program is a letter to the computer asking it to do something. Like any language, a programming language contains rules for its structure. And it uses a set of common words to convey the message.

There were (and still are) many different programming languages. An early language was FORTRAN which was short for formula translator. It was used mostly for mathematical problem solving. Another very easy to learn language was simply called BASIC. It was designed to make programming easy for college students just beginning to learn about computers.

By far the most utilized language during the mainframe era was COBOL. This contraction for COmmon Business Oriented Language explains itself. Each language had its own compiler program to convert the programmer's instructions into machine language.

By the way, in the Mainframe Era, the usual way to create a program was to first write out the instructions following the program language rules. Then the instructions were carefully punched into IBM cards. The only other choice would be to enter each instruction manually using the console switches located on the computer's front panel. But that also meant entering the instructions in the computer's machine language. That is exactly what CEs did.

A question may have entered your mind: What happens if a program deck was accidentally dropped? It was normally not the disaster you might imagine. The last few columns of each punch card usually contained a sequence number. After gathering up the mess (and hoping you found all the cards), the cards would be placed in an old gray iron machine called a card sorter. After a few passes, the deck would be good as new.

With knowledge of machine language, CEs were able to create short programs to aid in troubleshooting. CEs could also execute their programs one step at a time to watch the results of each instruction. Software really was an integral part of the mainframe mechanic's job.

Throw it all away

By the mid-1970s, knowing machine language became less important, yet software became even more entwined in the CE job. More diagnostic programs became available to aid in troubleshooting. Improvements to the customer's Operating System allowed it to generate some useful information about the condition of various machines. Perhaps it would help to think of the Operating System as Windows for Mainframes... but without the fancy graphics.

The improvemnts prompted IBM to try an experiment with some mainframe CEs to see if formal software training would help them do their jobs better. I was asked to attend the two month long software school in Kingston, NY. Before leaving, I was required to sign a non-disclosure agreement, because "you might be exposed to unannounced products while there."

The training was to be on the then current mainframe operating system, OS/VS1. The full name was Operating System/370 Virtual Storage, Systems Product Version 1. You can see why computer people prefer acronyms. This operating system was designed to utilize the virtual storage capabilities built into the System/370 hardware.

Our training was to include the structure of the operating system, the location of various information within the OS and how to interpret printouts of core functions. In other words, we would be capable of reading one of those huge stacks of paper that resulted from a "core dump." Following this training, we would be able to use that information to aid in troubleshooting computer system problems. We progressed through the material and actually began to understand the software side of computer systems.

Our Shrink

An added feature of this course was the presence of a very interesting psychologist I'll call Dr. Henry. He is remembered for his distinctive gravely, yet thin rather high-pitched voice. Mostly he wondered around observing. Just "hanging" with the guys. Occasionally he would interrupt with a short impromptu talk on some customer related issue.

Several weeks into our class, Dr. Henry announced that he would like to have each of us accompany him to another room where we would be asked to give a short bio-sketch of ourselves. There was an instant buzz as to the purpose. But he said it would give us confidence in presenting ourselves to customers.

When my turn came, I walked in and was warmly greeted. The room contained a small well-lit lectern stand. The rest of the room was semi-darkened, but you could see various equipment including a video monitor with 2 chairs off to one side. Dr. Henry sat in a chair just left of a large video camera that looked like it came from a TV studio. He asked me to just step up to the lectern and tell him a little about myself. Afterwards he would play back the recording and make suggestions for improving self-confidence.

About 2 sentences into my little speech, he stopped me and said, "You've done this before, right?" I admitted that I had done something similar in the past. I explained that I had attended an Army Instructor's School. He said, "OK, I don't think there is any problem here. Would you please send in the next guy?" It was amazing how fast he picked up on the previous experience. Later, I found out that he really did make suggestions to a couple CEs. And that was it. The subject was never mentioned again, although he remained with us to the end of the course.

Back to the course

Exactly half way through the course, as the Monday morning class began, our instructor asked us to gather up all the books, core dumps, notes, everything we had on our desks. Just outside the classroom door was a large bin. "Throw them all away;" he said. "We were about to begin a new phase and we no longer need any of those materials."

After we had dutifully cleared the tables, he asked us to step to the cabinets at the rear of the room. There we were to grab a fresh stack of books. As we did so, he explained that the first half of the course was merely to prepare us for what we would now study.

This was the real reason we were here. The new stack of books was for a different Operating System called MVS. This operating system added what might be called a super control program. It could host multiple virtual operating systems on one mainframe computer. It was like one of those beer commercials where a driver is controlling a large team of horses. It was definitely more complicated, but that first month had not been wasted. With what we learned initially, the pieces easily fell into place. A month later we really did learn to read those core dumps.

Party Time

As was tradition with training that lasted a month or more, the class got together for a "graduation party." After all, there is a certain camaraderie that builds after spending that much time together. Dr. Henry suggested a food and drink establishment down the road that led to Woodstock, NY. Dr. Henry and our instructor joined us for dinner, drinks and conversation on the evening before we were to complete the training and depart for home.

The following morning, our instructor noticed a missing class member. He asked around if anyone had seen Jerry. No one had. Not even Jerry's roommate at the hotel. Our instructor disappeared to make phone calls. He was in and out all morning since he was responsible for those in his class.

Around noon, Jerry came in looking under the weather, as they say. When asked where he had been, he said he had spent the night on Dr. Henry's living room sofa. His story was that he stayed quite late and saw Dr. Henry leave to go home. A couple minutes later, the good doctor came back inside saying he could not find his car. Thinking maybe it had been stolen, several people went outside... only to find the missing car parked right near the front door. With that, Jerry decided to drive the doctor home. The doctor's wife supplied a pillow and blanket for the sofa. Seen later in the day, the good doctor was in his characteristically good mood, smiling and showing no ill effects whatsoever. That made us realize that shrinks are just like us. Just one of the gang.

Hardware-Software Marriage

At the conclusion of the course we did find out that the non-disclosure agreements we signed were due to that second Operating System. It was still under development. It was eventually announced to the public a year later. In the meantime, we were instructed to not to reveal its existence. Also we were given special codes to use anytime we reported software related activity.

Apparently the experiment was successful. Eventually, another position was created in Field Engineering to address only the software aspects of computer systems. The Program Support Representative position was populated from within CE ranks. Software understanding was becoming more important to the overall understanding of system problems, even those involving only hardware.

In business, paperwork is a necessary evil. One such evil for CEs was the parts order form. It was required whenever repair parts or supplies were obtained from our parts center. The form was used often and everyone understood its necessity. But the most familiar form to every CE was the Incident Report. The "IR" actually originated back with Herman Hollerith. From day one it was the most important document in Field Engineering. Depending on what equipment we worked on and how difficult the repair, CEs completed anywhere from 1 to perhaps a dozen Incident Reports every day.

This might be a good place to clear up a misconception. CEs never responded to problems. Never. Sure, sometimes data went into a computer but ended up in the bit bucket. Occasionally spinning reels did not spin, etc. But we did not have problems. According to Mr. Hollerith, we experienced incidents. And that is the reason for Incident Reports. An IR was required for every problem (sorry incident) we encountered no matter how small. CEs came to hate the IR.

In the early days, Incident Reports came in a booklet form similar to a checkbook. Every machine had its own IR booklet. Not surprisingly, IR's were the size of an IBM card. The format included date, identification of the machine, codes categorizing the type of problem, more codes that described problem resolution and space for a comment or description of what was done to return the machine to operational status. Each IR had to be printed so the machine's carbon copy was legible.

Occasionally the comment was legible and helpful. CEs could be quite creative in their writing. The most common comment was "NTF" - no trouble found. Sometimes the letters were not in that order. Occasionally, we saw "MRSDI" - machine ran so did I. We all knew who that guy was, but I'm not telling. We all hated IRs.

Later, the Incident Report was "improved" to use optical character recognition technology which could be scanned for faster processing. It was faster for the accounting people, but much slower for CEs. We were required to learn how to print properly, legibly and within little boxes so the machines could read them. Naturally, the format was completely changed and it was now larger than an IBM card. It no longer fit a shirt pocket. To keep the forms from being folded, spindled or mutilated, we now carried an appropriately sized vinyl folder. Like a checkbook on steroids. Also, for speedy processing, these IRs had to be mailed daily. We hated IRs.

One Customer Engineer we worked alongside came from Hungary. Joe had been an Electrical Engineer back home, but immigrated to the US following the turmoil in his country in the 1960s. He fit right in with our culture. A great guy with an even greater work ethic. He held an excellent command of the English language, although when speaking to the ladies, somehow his accent seemed heavier. He said it usually worked. He loved every part of the job except the paperwork. Joe was often heard saying, "I go fix-it ma-cheen, you do-it paypa-verk." Did I mention we hated IRs?

Communication

Until the early 80s, whenever a customer encountered a problem, they phoned it in to a local dispatch center. The dispatcher would then page an appropriately trained CE, beginning with the CE responsible for that account. Our early pagers were really one-way radiophones. The radio frequency for all voice messages was the same, but a squelch function kept it quiet most of the time. The squelch was adjusted to the point where the background static and messages were muted. Each pager had a unique code so that only the designated pager would beep. When a page was received, the squelch was disabled so the message could be heard. A button on top was pressed to silence the pager following the message.

Occasionally during slow times, two or even three CEs would appear at an account for the same problem. To alleviate boredom, sometimes CEs would eaves drop by turning off the squelch. They heard all the messages, so repair became a group effort. Then it was off to lunch.

The brick

Around 1983, the next generation of communications came along. Our trusty pagers were replaced by the Data Communication

System or DCS (more acronyms). The DCS was a huge leap forward since we now had two-way digital communication with the dispatch office along with messaging capability and other uses. We all carried a Portable Terminal that featured a multi-line LCD screen and a full keyboard in a hand-held device about the size of a common brick... and about as heavy. Most of its weight was the battery which could power it for about 12 hours before charging was required.

The brick, as it became known, also replaced the Incident Report (Hooray!) and allowed ordering of parts, receiving parts delivery notices and such. It was an amazing communication device for its time. It would still be decades before other people knew what texting was all about. For the first time, CEs were independent of the telephone "land line."

Believe it or not, thirty-five years ago, there was a campaign to educate CEs on the evils of using the brick (texting) while driving. Although we joked heavily about the brick, the DCS really was a breakthrough in technology. If you would like to see more information on this technology, check the reference section at the end of the book.

Since CEs were salaried and treated well by the company, there was never talk of unions. No one felt a need for representation in labor-management discussions. There were however unions in other countries, but the very nature of unions outside the United States is considerably different. In other nations, unions might be better described as associations or benevolent societies. As an example, Adolph, a CE I met from Germany told me that in his country everyone was required to belong to a union. He confided that the majority of his salary went to the union. However, his union took care of all his obligations. They paid his mortgage, taxes, health, home, auto and life insurance. So the salary he took home was his to keep. Because of the different structure, labor strikes were nearly unheard of.

Although CEs were not unionized, they did deal with unions directly and indirectly through their customers. There were occasions where a customer's facility was picketed by a union. Members of other unions often joined in solidarity to harass those crossing a picket line. But management was always off limits.

There were occasions when CEs were asked to meet one of the customer managers at a shopping center or a nearby park. From there the manager would drive the CE onto the site, returning him to his car afterward. But generally we worked well with the union members.

Customers like Standard Oil of Ohio (SOHIO) had their headquarters located in a downtown building that required union electricians to do all electrical work. We were not allowed to connect power cords or lay the cables for installations. We still made all the connections within the machines. At Sohio, a CE would watch over and direct the union electricians during the process. It was never at our pace, but the job got done. More often than not, unions offered us amusement rather than grief.

Putting on a show

During the mainframe era, computer fairs or shows were frequently held to showcase the latest and greatest to potential customers. These shows tended to display smaller systems since they could be quickly and easily assembled and disassembled.

The first such show this CE was involved in was held in Cleveland's Public Hall, the largest part of which is located underground, under The Mall. The back wall of the lower exhibit hall was perhaps 30-35' high and formed an overlook of Lake Erie from the Mall above. The "back door" to the exhibit hall was located at one end of that wall. The entrance featured several huge doors that allowed semi-trucks to drive into and around inside the hall as necessary to unload their cargo.

Because the system destined for this show included several newly announced features, it was first delivered to our Data Center. There, it was completely installed and checked out in an open area just off the loading dock. The new the features were thoroughly tested to ensure there would be no surprises later. The system was then disassembled and loaded onto a flat-bed truck. The truck was not by choice.

The drivers for the logistics company we normally used were on strike. The only available truck was brought in. It was a flatbed rather than the usual box truck or semi-trailer. The weather was good and the distance was only a few miles, so it did not present a problem. The system was easily loaded off our loading dock. The driver had some difficulty securing the load to the truck bed, but with everything finally secured, he drove off.

Meanwhile, we drove to the hall entrance to meet the truck. When the driver arrived at the doors, a man greeted him and they talked for a minute. The driver then called us over. The greeter was another union driver employed by Public Hall. It seems only that particular union's drivers were allowed to drive inside the building. "Safety reasons." Our driver was told to get out of his truck and allow this other driver to take over. Our driver was upset because the truck and its contents were his responsibility. We negotiated a compromise where the hall's driver could drive, but our driver would accompany him as a passenger. With the truck safely inside, the local driver disappeared.

A clipboard carrying man approached to check us in and informed us that the unloading crew would be there shortly. Half an hour later, a forklift crew of four showed up. Two of them mounted the flat bed to loosen the tie-downs. The forklift operator and his director (for lack of a better term) remained off to the side. The first frame was moved to the edge of the truck bed. All the computer frames are on casters, so the forklift was able to easily maneuver under the frame. The crew checked to ensure the forks were properly positioned. As soon as the operator began to raise the lift, the rear wheels of the forklift cleared the ground as the whole thing tilted. The tips of the forks rested on the truck bed and prevented total disaster. The two workers on the truck reacted instantly to prevent the machine from tipping, but the frame hung at a precarious angle. Obviously it was way too heavy a load. They gently lowered the frame back to the truck bed. The crew then retreated promising to come back with a larger lift.

They returned about 45 minutes later with a much larger forklift. The unloading proceeded without incident. With our system on the floor, the unloading crew turned around and left. The truck was also free to return.

As we were about to start moving our machines to the designated area, another clipboard guy appeared. We were informed that we were not allowed to move any equipment inside the hall. Safety reasons, he said. Again we waited for the appropriate union people. A team of three arrived and chose to move the smallest frames first. These were 2311 Disk Drives which were roughly the size and weight of an ordinary dishwasher. The machine was not very heavy and the casters allowed it to be easily moved by one CE. In fact, CEs often took two at a time, pushing one and pulling the other. It was a different story here. Each machine required three union movers. With one of each side of the machine, the third guy walked in front announcing, "Watch out. Machine coming through. Watch out."

At the designated display area, we were allowed to assemble the system and connect all the interconnecting cables. That was because the union electricians wisely decided none of them knew how to do it. We still had to wait around for a union electrician to connect the power plugs, including an ordinary 110VAC extension cord. I was not present for the show or the aftermath, but I am sure the reverse procedure was similar.

The 2311 Disk Drive was only 40" high but held over 7 million characters of data.

Walking off the job

A year or so later we worked on another show at a different venue. Again the system was first assembled and tested at the Data Center. This was a smaller system and easily fit inside a box truck like the ones used to deliver appliances. This was our regular transport company, so all the machines were quickly loaded. The driver and two helpers headed to the grand ballroom of a downtown hotel. Once there, the unloading and moving into position was going smoothly. The unions at the hotel did not want responsibility for expensive computer equipment. They did not interfere with delivery or installation work by the various vendors.

Suddenly from one end of the room someone yelled, "Hey, what are you doing with our telephone equipment!" Half way across the room was one of our movers cradling a telephone in his hands. As two of the telephone workers headed toward him, he turned and quickly walked back out the door. He tossed the phone into the truck cab and stood guard in front of the door. The other two movers joined him. So there it was. A classic standoff. The telephone guys yelling that our movers stole telephone company property and the movers not saying a word. Outnumbered, the telephone guys retreated to the ballroom where they called for all the unions to walk off the job. Soon after, a telephone company car arrived with a couple supervisors. Not far behind was a moving company pickup with three burly reinforcements.

An hour later the forces that be worked out a settlement. If the telephone guys went back to our office and found a lone telephone in the room where our system had been, then the telephone union would admit that their guy must have been mistaken. What he saw must have been some computer equipment that just looked a lot like a telephone. Work resumed, albeit delayed almost two hours.

The Empty Room

The Cuyahoga River Valley runs through the city of Cleveland just west of the downtown area. Cuyahoga is a Native American word meaning crooked. And it is. Despite the river's twisting route, it is navigable for several miles. As a result, many industries took advantage of the location and its access to water and rail shipping. Traffic on the river included ore boats heading to steel mills from Minnesota mines. Some of them measured as much as one thousand feet in length. That, in turn led to the infamous Collision Bend. That is a story in itself, so more info is available in this book's reference section.

Even with the obvious obstacles, steel companies and other heavy industries could not pass up the protected location and huge amount of flat land. Jones & Laughlin Steel (which later merged with LTV Steel) owned prime property that was not very far up river. They located a large mill and their corporate offices along the river banks. When it became time to computerize the facility, the decision was made to build a new single story domed building to house their state of the art Data Processing Dept.

There were many delays in the construction, most of which involved various unions. Mostly the problems were over jurisdiction, with the steel workers' union wanting the work and local trade unions claiming their territory. The resulting delays meant the building was not ready when the new System/360 arrived. With nowhere to put the new computer, J & L negotiated space at our Data Center. The system was installed and J & L operators ran the system while couriers ferried input and output back to their headquarters facility.

When the building was finally completed, CEs packed up J & L's system and had it moved to the new Data Processing Building. The various machine frames were unpacked and positioned. Just as the CEs began to uncrate the cables, a union representative appeared and announced that the cabling was electricians' work. We would have to let the local union members do all the cable and connection work. J & L management, already tired of union caused delays, said no. Of course we agreed since the electricians knew nothing about our systems. The electricians vowed to shut down the entire facility. J & L immediately ordered the system repacked and moved back to the Data Center.

Negotiations went on for weeks, with IBM management brought in to consult. The J & L team finally agreed to allow the electricians to do the system install with two conditions. First, the union had to provide a cash bond against damage to the computer system in an amount equal to the cost of the system. That was close to two million dollars. Secondly, IBM required one trained CE to accompany each union worker to direct and supervise all work. And by the way, IBM would supply two CEs, the normal number required to do the installation. The union backed down when they decided it was not really worth the money just to make work for two members.

Yellow worms

Fisher Body (formerly a General Motors division) had a large factory on the east side of town. The facility was the typical layout for automotive plants. A hundred or so feet in front of the factory itself was a two story office building paralleling the plant and having a single story rather wide hall connecting the two. When the Fisher Body Division was dissolved in 1984, the site was converted into a huge automated warehouse. Lacking sufficient space in the office building for a computer room, General Motors decided to build a single story computer room adjacent to the interconnecting hallway. Once again, labor problems emerged and the computer room was nowhere near finished when the system arrived that autumn.

GM management decided to temporarily install the computer in their office cafeteria on the ground floor. This building was the old style office building with high ceilings and correspondingly tall windows. That was the prevalent design used before office buildings were air-conditioned.

We had a number of issues with this arrangement. There would be no raised floor since this was only temporary. Computer operators would be tripping over cables constantly. Therefore, cables had to be carefully routed to avoid operator work areas as much as possible and then bridges had to be constructed over the cables. Large capacity power connections needed to be installed. They too would be out on the open floor. GM reasoned that since it was almost winter and the new facility would be ready by spring, no air conditioning would be provided. With the windows being very tall, perhaps 10' high, they would simply open the tops and bottoms of the windows to allow air circulation. The customer insisted. The installation was completed.

All went according to plan until one of Lake Erie's famous "lake effect" snow squalls began blowing snow into the room. Operators quickly closed the windows. That was followed shortly thereafter by the system powering itself down due to a thermal condition. Computers do not play well with heat. Something had to be done, especially since further delays pushed the completion date for construction out into summer.

The greatest heat producer was the mainframe, followed by a couple of the control units. Management decided to install 24" fans at the top of several windows. Then, 24" diameter flexible hoses were attached to the fans and draped across the ceiling to where the control units were positioned. The hoses hung loosely several feet above the control units to suck the hot air directly outside.

The mainframe, with its greater heat load required extra attention. A thin plywood hood was fabricated to lay directly on top of the mainframe. It looked similar to the hoods found in restaurant kitchens. This one would directly draw the concentrated mainframe heat to the outside. The hoses swayed slightly as they drooped from their ceiling hangers. The room looked like there were huge yellow worms crawling across the ceiling. But it worked well enough to keep them going until the computer room was completed.

* * * * *

Fisher Body, as we still called it, was also one on those companies that was rather paranoid about industrial espionage. Cameras were forbidden anywhere on the premises. However, Sam, the account CE decided he just had to have a picture of that makeshift computer room with its big yellow worms.

One day he walked up to the front desk guard with a 35mm camera around his neck. As expected, the guard read him the riot act. Sam tried to explain that he only wanted a picture of the IBM equipment, and invited the guard to escort him to ensure no other pictures were taken. No wiggle room. Rules are rules. Reluctantly Sam took the camera back to his car and went about his business. Soon after he brought a miniature camera tucked away in his suit coat pocket. He proceeded to get the pictures he wanted.

Being the mischievous type, Sam snapped a clandestine view of the guard sitting at his desk talking on the telephone. I guess he just wanted to show that there was a way for a determined person to break the rules. This was back in the real film days. After the roll of film was developed and pictures printed, he carried the photo of the guard until onc day, the guard was not at his usual post. Sam dropped the photo on the guard's desk and left. The guard was absolutely positive that Sam was the culprit, but he could not prove it. Some CEs were not as innocent as they appeared.

9. Diversity

During the 1980s, various groups started calling for diversity in the workplace. IBM was often called out for being a "white boys club." That despite the company's having employed qualified people from all over the world and every known minority. Being an international company made that obvious. The operative word, of course, is qualified.

Employment had always been a matter of rigorous testing, interviews and even a physical. Throughout my career, I worked alongside black, Hispanic, Oriental and female CEs. I worked with a Hungarian refuge and even a Canadian. I have worked for women, blacks and Hispanics. We socialized and I called many friend. The problem was simply that there were not enough minority people qualified for the available jobs. Mostly that was due to lack of education, but also there were physical and personality issues.

The people in these diversity movements did not care. They chose to concentrate on raw numbers rather than qualifications. They pushed for hiring quotas. So, under intense pressure, IBM began concentrating on hiring only minorities. At first testing was reduced to allow more to qualify and then testing was eliminated completely. Some of the resulting hires were very good. Others were total disasters.

A typical 1960s computer room.

I can honestly say I never ran across a truly prejudiced person in all those years. Well, there was one exception. That Hungarian refuge CE absolutely hated Russians. Actually, there was only one thing to which every CE was passionately opposed – incompetence.

Cabling

Bear with me a moment as we need to supply some additional background again. Whenever you see a photo of a computer system, the machines stand at attention on a pristine floor in a brightly lit room. Publicity shots. What you do not see is what goes on beneath the machines. Many people do not realize that those machines stand on a false floor that is usually 12-18" deep. Some floors were exceptions, like being deep enough to crawl around on your hands and knees, but those were rare.

The false floor construction is a sturdy steel framework laid out in 2 foot squares and held up by dozens, or even hundreds, of adjustable stanchions. This framework requires carefully leveled before the steel reinforced tiles were laid in place. Tiles are always finished with a layer of vinyl for appearance. Besides hiding the maze of cables required for power and communication between the machines, the raised floor acts as a plenum for air conditioning.

IBM SYSTEM/360 PARALLEL CHANNEL CABLE - 15 Foot (4.6 m)
one of two (Bus and Tag) required per Channel
400 feet (122 m) maximum length of cable pair

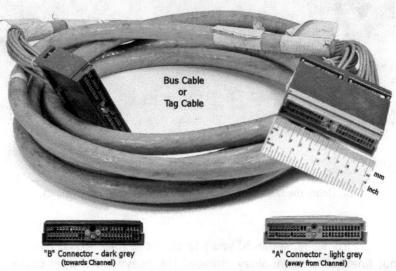

Bus Cable
or
Tag Cable

"B" Connector - dark grey
(towards Channel)

"A" Connector - light grey
(away from Channel)

Each component of a mainframe computer system required at least 4 cables. Machine power was supplied through a 30 to 60 ampere power cord roughly two inches in diameter. There was a small half inch cable for an Emergency Power Off safety system. Finally, communication between machines required a minimum two more one and a half inch diameter cable bundles called "channel cables." Each channel cable contained a couple dozen wires that carried data and control information. Channel cables could be as long as 400' and weigh over one hundred pounds. Obviously installing or changing these cables was not a task for a "ninty-eight pound weakling."

In attempts at diversity, our office hired several people who were obviously not physically qualified. It was a sad and sorry sight to see them struggle with the unwieldy loads. For them it could also be an impossible task just positioning a computer frame during an installation. All the desire in the world did not translate into a good experience for them.

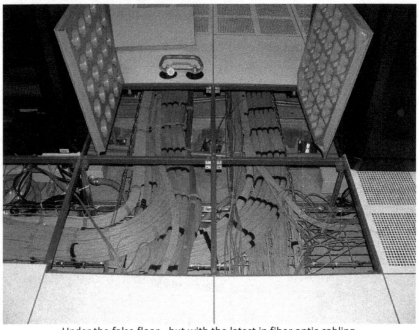

Under the false floor - but with the latest in fiber optic cabling.

Ironically, some 30 years later, these folks would have worked out fine. Later technology replaced the heavy old copper cables with fiber optics. What had been an inch and a half diameter cable was replaced by a three-eighths inch fiber optic cable.

Rookie Routine

While waiting for their initial Basic Training Course, new hires were usually sent to various larger accounts for week long orientations. Basically the new employee was told, "Go observe and see if you can lend a hand." The rookies also helped to install new systems, which gave them an idea of the dirty part of the job. The next step was to shadow one or more CEs until a slot at Basic School was available. That usually meant another week or two accompanying a CE who covered multiple smaller accounts.

During the time I was assigned the National City Bank's Data Center, several rookies came our way. One that comes to mind was James. He was a tall, good looking and confident young man. During his week with me, he was ever alert and eager to help. He pitched in and was not afraid of getting his hands dirty.

Once, during a quiet time, I asked James how he had decided to join IBM and what aspects of Field Engineering interested him most. He said that he had seen an ad in the local newspaper, so he thought he'd check it out. He added that he was going to be a manager. I responded that this was an excellent target for down the road, but what about his immediate future? But somehow he was convinced he was going to be a manager. There was not much conversation after that.

About two weeks later, I got word that James was off to CE Basic School. A week after that I was told he washed out after only three days. Unfortunate. He had a great attitude and was equally ambitious, but lacked the basic technical skills right from the start. He was one of many hired and fired during that time. Much time and money was spent trying to fill those quotas.

Another Rookie

Janet was an athletic young lady with a pleasant outgoing personality. She was not afraid to work hard or dirty her hands. Actually, she understood much of the job because she was following in her father's footsteps. Dad had been a CE since the old gray iron days.

She had grown up watching her father fix things around the house and work on the family car.

I had one small difficulty with Janet when she first started. She smoked. I had warned her up front that computer rooms, including adjacent rooms like our little office, were no smoking areas. NCB, as did most customers, protected their computer equipment with sensitive fire detection systems that could automatically flood the area with CO_2 to extinguish any fire that might occur. These systems included sensors at the ceiling level and beneath the false floor. If any two sensors detected smoke, an alarm was sounded and everyone had 30 seconds to evacuate the area.

Once while she was doing her initial "follow the CE" routine, we were sitting in the CE Room. At side by side desks, we talked as I completed some paperwork. Not thinking, she pulled out a cigarette and lit it.

As it happened to be, the middle drawer of my desk contained a pair of the longest scissors I had ever seen. The blades were about a foot long. I had no idea as to their purpose or from whence they came. They were in the drawer when I arrived at the account. Anyway, I grabbed them, reached over and cut her cigarette in half as she held it. Startled, she stared at me for a few seconds and then, realizing what she had done, began laughing. She said, "I can't believe you did that." I replied, "Neither can I." But she never lit up again.

It is noteworthy that Janet was still on the job when I retired and eventually retired as her father had done.

The new manager

One day I was on the phone with my manager discussing his planned visit to my account. As we spoke, suddenly he said, "Damn. I forgot. I can't do it tomorrow. I've got rookie duty."

The normal office routine was that each Field Manager rotated being the Duty Manager of the day. As such, he was responsible for any incoming calls that required a management decision and also filling in for any manager who was out of the office that day. The Duty Manager also handled customer inquiries and complaints.

Rookie duty was different. This was a special case involving a new Field Manager in our office. When it was her turn to be the duty manager, one of the other managers was assigned to guide her and prevent problems that might affect the office. This particular rookie needed much guidance.

Jill had been hired on the basis of her bachelor of business degree majoring in finance. She was being fast-tracked for advancement due to the perceived lack of female managers. She had to follow the usual path, but faster than the usual pace of 3-6 months per step. The procedure involved being moved through various positions so as to understand those jobs, company structure and the business in general. In less than one year, she was now a Field Manager. Her only computer experience had been as a computer user while earning her business degree.

The story of her progress was later related by my manager. First, Jill became an office specialist were she answered phones and did various administrative jobs around our branch office. Jill was then assigned as a CE. No need for training as she would only shadow a CE. Like any rookie CE, she was issued a "toolbag" and asked to help as necessary. Our tools were carried under the guise of a briefcase... that weighted about thirty pounds. An immediate problem was the tools where too heavy for her to carry. Therefore she was assigned to a large multiple CE account where carrying tools was not required. She proved to be incapable of assisting with any physical labor. After a couple months watching CEs work, she was assigned as a Program Support Representative. That, despite her never having had any training or understanding of computer programming. Shortly after that she was off to Field Manager School where she did well.

Jill was intelligent and educated, but lacked the ability to manage. After about 3 months of rookie duty and every Field Manager in the office ready to revolt, Jill was promoted to a job with the Area staff in Detroit. Less than 12 months after that, she was back shuffling paperwork with the office accounting staff. Rumor was the Area Manager sent her back saying, "You hired her, you fire her." Despite the obvious lack of ability in this job, no one wanted to fire her for fear of a discrimination lawsuit. She finally tired of the menial tasks that were assigned and quit. Again, the attempt at filling a quota put a huge demand on company resources, especially our office. I am sure she did well in the right job, but what a costly distraction while in the wrong job.

During that mainframe era, we crossed paths and worked with some of the most intelligent, talented, dedicated and diverse people to be found on the planet. The same descriptions can be applied to most of our customers as well. Sure, there were a few nasty folks, but we'll ignore that small number. Also a few of these people may have been interesting in the old Chinese curse sense of the word. These are just a few of those memorable people.

The Parts Room Guy

As one might expect, we had a local parts room that stocked the thousands of mechanical and electronic parts needed in our work. They stocked everything from nuts, bolts and rags to complex assemblies costing many thousands of dollars.

The traditional method of tracking the parts inventory was with IBM cards. These inventory cards were organized by part number and filled huge trays immediately opposite the pickup counter. In addition to the part number, each card contained a location and the quantity on hand. Parts personnel updated the on-hand quantity as they distributed the part.

The procedure for obtaining a part was to first phone in to verify the part was in stock. With part number in hand, the parts man would find the proper card among the numerically sequenced cards and check the number in stock. If they were out of stock, the card would be missing as it was pulled out to order more. If the part was in stock, the employee would fill out a parts requisition, update the stock quantity, and then "pull" the part. In addition to the part number and quantity, the requisition required the CE's name, his ID number, and the verification of a security code, which was different for every office and changed monthly. Complicated, but it worked. Mostly.

The parts room often hired college students for part-time work, especially during summer vacation times. Gary was one such student. Actually, he had taken the fall semester off, so he was available to continue work during the day shift. His memory was absolutely amazing.

The first time Gary took your parts order, the procedure was followed normally. The next time you called for a part, the conversation was very short. It went something like this:

"Parts room, Gary"

"Hi Gary. I need a part."

"Oh, hello John, what do you need?"

"I need a *doflochy*."

"How many?"

"Just one."

"You better make it two. We found some bad ones in stock."

"OK, make it two"

"You got it! Bye."

When you arrived, your parts were waiting in a bag with a copy of the requisition form stapled to it. Every line filled in correctly. Every time. Gary was hired full-time at night as he continued his education. He eventually graduated and was immediately hired as a Systems Engineer.

Systems Engineers were kind of super programmers who worked for the marketing division. Their job was to ensure all the customer software and operating procedures worked properly with any new computer system. That's not all Gary did. There was his side job as a professional musician who played the local bars and clubs on weekends. Needless to say, we sorely missed his amazing memory when he left the parts room.

Later on the parts inventory was computerized to a database system that was accessed through video terminals. That made the job much easier for the rest of the people working in the parts room. Still later the system was further automated to the point that we could order parts from our DCS portable terminals (the "bricks").

CE to Butcher

Harry was a quiet sort of guy. An excellent CE. But he never joined the guys for a quick one after work. It was not that he was a loner. Not by any means. He just seemed to be busy all the time. Eventually, his secret life was revealed. He was building a house on an acre of land he bought in an eastern fringe suburb. He was not building his house as in hiring a contractor and giving him a set of plans. Harry was literally building almost everything himself. The only things he contracted out were some masonry and cement work and the heating system. The rest he did himself with the help of his wife and kids.

The details of Harry's house project would fill a book in itself. To give you an idea of how much he did on his own, the first thing he did was buy a used backhoe. That was used to dig the foundation and install a septic system. He custom made all the windows in his current garage. With the help of his family, he raised the walls and did the roofing. When the house was complete, he landscaped the yard and sold the backhoe.

The finished product was a gorgeous ranch finished in fieldstone by the Amish stonecutter he hired. I asked Harry if this would be his retirement home. He said no, this house was good for now, but it was just practice. Shortly after his family moved in, he sold the old house and bought several acres of land just over the Pennsylvania-Ohio border. True to his word, he started over again. This time he began by buying a used RV trailer in which to stay while he worked. Weekends and vacations were spent on his project.

While working on his house, Harry got to know the people of a nearby town quite well. After all, it took some years before it was ready to move in. Harry had over 20 years with the company so a retirement income was assured. Then, still in his 50s, he quit his CE job and moved the family to Pennsylvania. He went to work for the local grocery/butcher store. He knew the owner was thinking of retiring in a few years. Harry learned all about the business including butching. The last time I ventured over there, Harry's Market was doing well. He loved the laid back lifestyle. Especially no more middle of the night call-outs for him.

The Tool Guy

Bob was one of the old-timers in the office. A veteran CE, who had been around since the before the Mainframe Era. Having been around that long, he was one of the first to receive training on those new-fangled computer machines. He really enjoyed the new technology and learned all he could. He became the first computer specialist in the office.

Despite his role in the world of electronics, he had always been fascinated by tools. Bob just plain loved tools. He had at least one of everything. That included electrical, automotive, carpentry, masonry, plumbing and even farm tools. His collection included antique as well as current tools. Whenever anyone had a question about tools, it was, "ask Bob."

Sharing of his tools was never a problem. When asked to borrow a tool, the usual answer was, "which one?" Chainsaw sharpener: power or files? Wheel balancer: dynamic or static? He was a great resource to all and respected enough that people always returned the borrowed tool.

Narrow Territory

As mentioned earlier, at IBM schools we generally paired with a CE in the course. Unless two CEs from the same office were attending the same school, your roommate was luck of the draw. I can honestly say there was never a bad draw. I found each roommate to be friendly and most interesting. We usually discussed our home offices, our territories, the company, etc. Classmates often ate suppers together in small groups at nearby restaurants. And groups of CEs were often found at local establishments quenching their thirsts. On weekends, we often made joint excursions to visit local attractions.

One of my more memorable roommates was Jacques. His office was located in Quebec City, QC but he lived in Sept Iles, Quebec. He described it as a city of twenty thousand people situated on a bay along one of the wider sections of the St. Lawrence River. It was named for seven small islands just offshore. It was also over six hundred miles from his branch office. He enjoyed working from his home and seldom visited the office. Likewise, he seldom had visitors from Quebec City. A car buff, he was most proud of the "Zed 28" parked in his driveway. Most people won't have much trouble translating that from the French-Canadian language.

Jacques was assigned what was known as a resident territory. It consisted of 3 major customer accounts, each with a System/360 computer. There were also a few miscellaneous machines around town. The obvious question was what type of companies located in a small town in such a remote area? He explained the accounts were actually three lumber camps, all located north of the city. The closest was around 250 kilometers (155 miles) away. His farthest customer was almost 600 kilometers (375 miles) due north. He laughed and in his heavy French accent, said, "My territory is six hundred kilometers long and the width of the railroad track." Absolutely true. There were no highways heading that far north. The only major highway thru the town went east and west following alongside the St. Lawrence River. Travel to the north was by train or logging roads.

Twice a week, the train added a combination passenger and mail car. That was to accommodate the lumberjacks heading to or from their month long stays at the camps. He described each camp as a mini-city, much like a military post. Each had offices, sleeping quarters, a mess hall, a movie theater, recreation rooms and guest quarters. He said it was like staying in a cheap hotel but with complete maid service. When he headed north, he would stop at each camp to do scheduled maintenance and fix any problems they had accumulated since his last visit. This normal maintenance routine would see him gone two to three weeks before returning home.

Emergencies were another story. Depending on the season, he would travel via pontoon or ski plane. By necessity, each logging camp was located on a lake, so quick access was not all that difficult. The only real drawback he found was in the time necessary to obtain repair parts. That was measured in days or weeks as opposed to our norm of minutes to hours. Jacques said he enjoyed the freedom of no set hours. No argument there. I remember thinking it sounded like a great place to retire. We lost touch, but I'll guess he is retired too and still living in the same house.

Not all machines were located in computer rooms. Before computers, the so called data processing machines could be located most anywhere. Even with the advent of the mainframe, the input/output or peripheral machines might be located in a different room or even on an adjacent floor. Often machines were connected remotely to the computer by phone. All contributed to the adventure of the job.

Out back

As a rookie back in 1966, my initial assignment was working on "card" machines. There were hundreds of keypunch machines and card sorters all over town. Surprising for mechanical machines, they ran very well. Among our customers were a number of small companies that provided keypunch services to other companies. Basically they handled overflow work or contracted with companies too small to have their own data processing department.

Responding to a call at one such company lead to an older residential neighborhood. There was no sign visible at the given address. Up the short walk and up onto the front porch of a 1920s bungalow where I rang the bell. A middle-aged lady in jeans and a casual top answered the door. I asked if she had placed a call for service. She said yes and asked me to follow her. We walked down the hall past a normal looking living room and dining room then into the kitchen. From there we proceeded out the back door onto a very large enclosed porch. There along the porch walls were two keypunch machines and a card verifier. One of the keypunches required some adjustment to its print unit. At that time there were many similar entrepreneurial opportunities for those so inclined.

The card verifier machine has not been mentioned before. It was a machine that could easily be mistaken for a card punch. Mechanically they were identical to a keypunch except the punching unit was replaced with a mechanism that sensed the presence of punched holes. After a card was punched, it was placed in the verifier and the identical characters were keyed in again. If any of the characters did not match, the card was rejected and sent back to be re-punched.

Planted machines

The size of our customers' facilities varied tremendously. Some were very small as the one in the previous story. Others were located in factories where hardhats were required or in automated warehouses where it was necessary to evade the driverless carts. Still others were secure government locations where you were escorted by armed guards.

The one common factor for each customer was the composition of their computer room. Large or small, the computer room was different from other spaces. In the last chapter we exposed the ugly truth under the floor, but let me elaborate a bit. Wherever a system component frame was located, holes had to be cut into the tile below to allow the power and interconnecting cables to emerge. The holes were always located under the machine frame, so they are never seen in photos. Each machine had to be "planted" with wheel locks or small built-in jacks to prevent their moving. It was not pretty when a machine caster rolled into a hole.

Normally, access to the false floors was only required during installations or removals. This was not like your living room. Rearranging the "furniture" in a computer room was not a simple task.

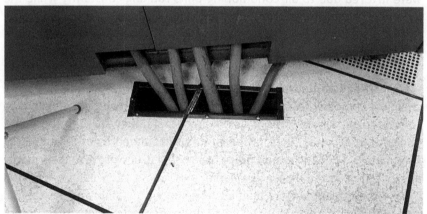
A machine moved slightly to reveal its cabling.

When an additional machine frame was added to a system, things got complicated. Since each frame was firmly planted on the tiles, only certain other tiles could be removed. It all had to be planned.

Special care was necessary when it came to power connectors which needed to be readily accessible for the obvious reasons. Furthermore, the interconnecting channel cables were often daisy-chained from one machine to the next. On occasion such a chain sequence was rearranged for better operation. Makes it obvious that CEs had no need for health club memberships. Their workouts were included in the job.

The Cable Mole

Once in a while we ran into non-standard false floors. There was a utility company that located its computer complex in a distant suburban area for security reasons. The former farm allowed the specifically designed building to be located far off the road. The building had a huge computer room located in the center of the basement. Above ground were the offices and other facilities.

For some unknown reason, the false floor was approximately three feet deep. Unusual, but it was great for us! One CE would be designated "the cable mole." From one opening, he would be handed a cable and pointed in the correct direction. On hands and knees (gloved and padded of course), he dragged the cable to its destination where his head would pop out of a hole. Yes, just like "Caddy Shack." By the way, when we did installation work, we wore work clothes. Jeans, a flannel shirt and a pair of gloves were the uniform of the day. Flannel shirts were favored due to air-conditioning units running constantly while the disconnected machines were not producing any heat.

Not on the level

The most unusual raised floor ever encountered was at a small chemical company located in the city. When the company decided to computerize their operations, like many others, they realized there was no room to expand. Their property was surrounded by other industrial companies. There was no choice but to build upward. And, the only appropriately sized space available was above a previous addition behind their headquarters building. The lower building was now a vital part of the plant operation and could not be moved or even interrupted. The solution was to build over the old structure. Steel posts and framework were installed above the older building so as to match the third floor of their existing office building. The computer room and false floor was built on the framework.

The resulting computer room appeared to be an absolutely normal third floor room. All the old floors matched the new raised floors without ramps of any kind. The surprise came when you lifted out one of the floor tiles. That old building I mentioned? It was a slanted "shed" roof building. At one end, the floor depth was maybe a foot. The other end required a ladder. Obviously all the cables could not be allowed to dangle that far down, so cable troughs were built to relieve the strain.

Love the Job

The two-foot square tiles used in raised flooring systems were usually ignored unless there was an installation in progress. When access was required, a Floor Panel Pulling Tool was used. (One can be seen near the top of the second Chapter 9 photo.) It consisted of two heavy duty suction cups attached to a handle with levers to release the suction when necessary. To us they were simply "floor suckers."

At one account, we discovered that trying to remove a tile resulted in lifting the decorative vinyl surface only. The tiles were defective due to the glue not bonding properly to the steel under-panel. The floor suckers worked only on the smooth vinyl, not the rougher steel underneath. The only means of opening this floor was to pry at the edges of a tile or by starting at a tile containing a cut hole. After that, each successive tile needed to be pushed up from underneath. For us it was a major problem. The customer ignored the problem because of the disruption it would cause to operations as well as the costs involved. The situation came to a head when one of their employees slipped and fell on a loose tile.

The company hired a man to come in and re-cement each piece of vinyl back in place. The fellow they hired, named Jack, was a muscular young man who always seemed to be in need of a shave. He came in each morning with his tools and a lunch bucket. Most mornings he was very quiet and did not seem to be quite awake. Dutifully, he lifted each piece of vinyl, cleaned it and the steel base, then re-glued the tile in place with some sort of contact cement. This was followed by a thorough rolling with a small but heavy roller. We raised various machine supports and slightly moved some frames so he could do his job. It took him close to two weeks to get the whole room done. Funny thing. By afternoon, Jack could be heard singing away, happy with his job. Great stuff that contact cement.

Under construction

While working the Saturday schedule we had the opportunity to visit customer sites all over the city. Of course this was way before GPS and cell phones. All we had were city maps to find customer locations.

One Saturday morning a disk drive error call came in from a company known as Bank Systems Corp. They were an early clearing house for credit card purchases. I was given an address, as usual. It was on a main artery in a near west side suburb. However, I could not find the address. The closest building at only two digits off was a Denny's restaurant. Frustrated, I went into the Denny's and called our dispatcher. He verified the address given. I told him it simply did not exist. The dispatcher called the customer on another line and we had a three way conversation. The customer supervisor asked me where I was. I told him I was in a Denny's restaurant. He said, "Good. Can you see out the back of Denny's?" Peeking around the corner from the phone, I could. He continued, "Do you see a building behind Denny's that is under construction?" I did. "That's us, we're in the basement." He added that eventually there would be a driveway next to the restaurant.

I grabbed my tool case and walked across the dusty ground that would someday be a parking lot for the future three story office building. There were poured concrete floors with a central core containing elevator shafts, stairways and what I assumed would eventually be rest rooms. But there were literally no outside walls anywhere. Nothing but the poured concrete floors held up by a sea of supporting steel columns. I walked to the center where the elevator shafts were blocked by X's made of 2x4s. Alongside the shafts was a stairway leading to the basement. At the bottom of the stairs were hung bare light bulbs. Only the immediate area was cemented. Beyond was only mud, illuminated by a few scattered bare bulbs dangling from the ceiling. At the opposite end of the cement island next to an elevator shaft was a solitary gray metal door. I tried the knob and it opened. Stepping in and up a couple steps put me on the computer room floor. There, a very normal looking computer room hummed away and people were about their business.

As I walked toward the first office, I was met by a man who asked, "Are you the IBM guy?" The first thought that came to mind was, what a dumb question. Who else would be wearing a suit and carrying a brief case on a Saturday morning... and in the basement of an unfinished building. I held my tongue.

An apology was made for the delay in finding the place. He was not concerned. "Happens all the time. At least they finally put the sign on the door." "Sign?" I asked, "didn't see a sign." He went out to check and sure enough, it was gone. The masking tape holding a piece of printout paper with a big "IBM" scribbled on it had come loose. Apparently the breeze blowing through the open building had taken it out into the muddy darkness.

About a year later, another Saturday call brought me back to Bank Systems. By then the building was a gleaming office building with beautiful landscaping and a paved parking lot. For security reasons the data center was not listed on the directory, but I knew exactly where it to find it.

Incognito

Back in the 70s and 80s, way before terrorist concerns, a few of our customers were already paranoid about security. CEs expected tight security at the government facilities we serviced like NASA or the Navy Finance Center. One customer stood out as having the most secretive and secure facility in the area.

That company was Service Bureau Corporation, which was actually a wholly owned subsidiary of IBM. As the name implies, they were a service bureau. They existed solely to supply computing services to other companies. SBC had sites in a number of cities, but this one was their worldwide teleprocessing center. It was located near the center of Lakewood, Ohio, a western suburb of Cleveland. Studies had shown this location had the most reliable telephone service in the country. And there was a fire station literally across the street. SBC occupied the second floor and basement of the corner office building. They also occupied the basement of another large building next door. Both buildings contained retail space on the first floor and offices above. There were no signs in building directories, save a single entry which listed the SBC second floor office.

In the basement sanctuary were located eight large IBM 360 systems. They were all alike and connected in a unique configuration that allowed any one of them to control the remaining seven systems. A separate room housed dozens and dozens of disk storage machines. There were separate rooms filled with telephone equipment. All power and phones lines entered underground. There was even a large battery and inverter room to power the equipment long enough (less than a minute) to allow the emergency diesel generators out back to kick in. All exits were alarmed and stairs and hallways were video monitored.

Entrance to the computer area was via the one key enabled elevator that went to the basement or by an unmarked stairway door at the back of the building lobby. Both lead down to a hallway containing a number of unmarked doors. The entry door to the computer area required card entry and was guarded 24/7. There was also a secret stairway that lead exclusively from the basement to the 2nd floor offices.

Extreme? Perhaps. But SBC management often reminded us, "If the computers are down, we're out of business." Faster and more abundant communication lines as well as reduced cost of owning a computer system eventually killed the teleprocessing and service bureau businesses. Hundreds of such businesses departed the scene years ago. But in their day, they were highly profitable.

Second floor of the closet

Banks have always tried to project a grand image of security and safety. No exception was the main office of National City Bank in the Garfield Bldg. in downtown Cleveland. It boasted two full banking floors. Each floor was really 2 stories high. Marble columns, genuine red mahogany paneling and huge brass chandeliers to provide light. A long row of teller windows with their ornate brass fences stretched across one side of the floor. Near the opposite wall were a row of standup desks with classic green shaded lights where customers could fill out deposit slips and the like. Very impressive. That left approximately half the floor space for customers to line up at the Teller windows. On most weekdays, both floors were busy with customers.

When the age of video terminals arrived, NCB was among the first to modernize with teller terminals. The computer room was not near the banking floors, but there was a solution with a remote video terminal control unit that could communicate with the mainframe through telephone lines. That was all well and good, but where to locate that control unit was a problem. It was beyond the bank's image to have a brightly colored machine the size of 2 refrigerators sitting out in plain sight on a banking floor.

The solution was truly unique. On the upper banking floor, along the wall behind the teller windows were several doors hidden in the mahogany paneling. Behind those doors were break rooms, teller counting rooms and the like. One of the doors led to a tiny hall containing three more doors. The door straight ahead was labeled Men. To the right was the appropriately labeled janitorial closet. To the left was an unmarked closet/storage room approximately five feet square. Building plans indicated that the area above these rooms was unfinished space. NCB maintenance people broke through the closet ceiling to verify the existence of the unfinished area. There was more than sufficient space for the control unit, but it was inaccessible and there were no lights or power. The real problem was no way to get a machine into that space.

Their solution was expensive, but not a problem for the bank. First a large spiral staircase was installed in the closet. A sizable room was created over the hallway, rest room and janitor's closet. When finished, it included lighting, power, telephone lines and its very own air conditioner. For access, the upper portion of the banking floor paneling was removed and a set of double doors were installed in the wall. A sliding I-beam hoist was installed in the ceiling to lift the machine into place. Finally the original paneling was carefully reinstalled so that the doors were barely noticeable, if you knew where to look.

There it was: the only IBM machine ever installed on the second floor of a closet. Most of us had no problem but claustrophobic CEs were excused from working on it.

Rickety Stairs

Here is another short tale of 2nd floor doors. There was a large bearing distributor in town. They sold many types and sizes of bearings from huge wheel size down to tiny motor bearings. Their local warehouse and office was located in an old brick structure with wooden floors from the turn of the century – the previous one. Being in a city environment, the building walls were built inches from the property line so as to maximize the floor space.

From the front entrance, past the receptionist, through an office area was a centrally located wooden stairway leading to the second floor. The well-worn stairs creaked loudly as they were climbed. The data processing department resided on the 2nd floor at the right-rear of the building. It was a long walk when carrying a thirty pound tool case, but CEs are used to that.

Actually, I was not aware of the facility until the company decided to install a computer to replace their old gray iron – the old tabulating machines. Since the only stairway was too fragile, the older machines had been raised to the 2nd floor by a crane positioned in the open lot next door. A set of double doors had been cut into the side wall of the second floor for that purpose. The company thought the same fifty-year-old doors could be used for the upgrade. There was a slight problem. A hotel had been built next door. Fortunately the doors now opened over the hotel's temporary parking area, not onto a blank wall.

I have no idea what it cost, but the distributor negotiated the blocking of a major portion of the hotel parking lot for a crane and trucks to deliver the new equipment. They had to repeat the operation later to remove the old tabulating equipment once the conversions were completed.

12 – Fun Fixes

Bell ringer

Back in the late 60s, one of our accounts was Richman Brothers Clothing. They were a manufacturer of men's suits, both custom and ready-made. Their computer was a System 360 model 30, which was "card based." It used decks of punched cards to load in various programs and data. I was never assigned to the account, but I had been there more times than I care to remember. It was part of our group's territory. A fellow CE shared this story from around 1968.

The customer became very upset because their system's card reader kept failing. They said CEs had been out a number of times but could never find the problem. Without the card reader working, none of the programs could be run.

Ray, the account CE, had not been aware of any problem because there had been any problems while he was onsite during the day. He pulled out the machine log book and sure enough there had been 4 or 5 calls placed on that machine. Then he noticed that each call was after midnight on a Friday or Saturday night. Ray discussed this with Richman Brothers management and they realized all the calls had been placed by one particular operator. They wondered if he had been using these calls as a way to catch a nap.

Richman's Data Center Manager came up with a solution. The System/360 Model 30 had an "alarm" that could be programmed to sound using a software command. The alarm was actually a small bell about twice the size of the bells atop antique wind-up alarm clocks. He had one of his programmers force the computer to sound the alarm every 30 minutes after midnight on weekends. No calls were received for the next couple weekends. The card reader was fixed by terminating the operator's employment.

The computer of many colors

The System/360 was available in six colors. The most popular ones were Classic Blue, followed closely by Garnet Rose. No matter what it was called, it was RED. There was a Sunshine Yellow that required sunglasses and for old-time's sake, Pebble Gray (the color of "old Gray Iron".) I never did see the other two colors of Willow Green and Charcoal Brown in customer offices, but they were sighted on several internally used machines. Normally a company ordered their entire computing system, including all the peripheral equipment in the same color. It made for a very impressive display.

In my travels, I remember only one exception to the coherent color standard. That was at the Navy Finance Center. Amongst other functions, NFC was where the monthly checks for retired Navy personnel were printed. The first time I was called there, I kept thinking that the place looked like a circus tent. There were two printers, one red and one blue. There were two card reader/card punch machines, one red and one blue. There were rows of tape drives in red, yellow and blue. The mainframe and control units were all three. I repaired the problem they were having, but before I left, I had to know the reason for all the different colors. Initially, I thought that perhaps the system had been cobbled together from pieces of other systems.

Trying to be funny, I asked the supervisor, "What's with all the colors? Were they on sale?" She didn't think it was that funny. She said, "Follow me." I followed her to the computer console. There, she opened a book labeled Job Run Procedures to a random page. I was invited to read what was there:

Job# USN0391-4
1. Put single-part 11"x 14" paper in the blue printer.
2. Place card deck RB0391 in the red card reader.
3. Mount tape #10083 on a blue tape drive.
4. Mount 2 scratch tapes on yellow tape drives.
Etc.

No, I do not remember the exact text. My memory was never that good. But that is close to the way their program run instructions were written. She explained civilian government employees ran the center, but sailors were assigned to them as operators and assistants. Normally, the sailors were rotated through every 6-12 months. Therefore taking the time to properly train each sailor was counter-productive. It made sense after all. A truly embarrassing moment for which I profusely apologized.

Long lines

Actually there are two stories about the same account. This company was a supplier of scientific equipment and laboratory supplies. Their home office was located in Pennsylvania. A satellite warehouse and its associated office were opened in our area due to the large medical community in Cleveland.

Their system was set up to allow purchase orders received at either office to be filled by the closest warehouse. Also, if an item happened to be out of stock, the item could be shipped from the other warehouse. At our end, the only equipment necessary was a control unit with video terminals and a couple of small printers. The control unit communicated with the home office via telephone lines. At the time it was called teleprocessing. The machine they used was actually the same type as we mentioned before in use at National City Bank. This very small account was assigned to me because I was the only trained CE with other accounts nearby.

The remote control unit managed the printers and some first generation video terminals. Communication to the home computer site was in "full duplex" mode, which utilized two standard telephone lines. Both lines were necessary for correct operation since one line was dedicated to incoming data, while the other carried only outgoing data. One day the customer reported they were not able to send or receive any orders. Once on site, it did not take long to determine the problem lay with the incoming phone line.

At that time, all long distance calling was handled by the AT&T Long Lines Division rather than the local Ma Bell office. I placed a service call to Long Lines. A telephone guy arrived within the hour. He seemed to be having trouble understanding the problem. He finally admitted the regular Long Lines repairmen were all busy, so they sent him and he was not really familiar with this "full duplex thing." I tried, as best I could to explain that our problem was we were not receiving any data on the one line. Just when I thought he finally understood, the phone guy reached out and pulled the two line plugs out, reversed them and plugged them back in. "There, try it now," he said. Calmly I replied, "It still doesn't work." "Well how do you know, you haven't tried it yet?" I said, "Reversing those two lines means that now we can't send any data because the outgoing line is bad." Shaking his head, he went

91

out to call for backup. It took almost another hour for a real Long Lines Repairman to arrive. This guy knew exactly what to do. After coordinating a change of lines with his central office, the customer was operational again.

My other story about this company involves their office manager, Skip. He was the sort of guy who was always in a good mood even during not so good times. At a much later date, Skip called in mid-afternoon saying the remote control unit was failing. Once on site, I spent a fruitless hour trying to diagnose the problem so I called for assistance from a specialist. By then, Skip had sent his employees home for the day since without the system, they had nothing to do. Skip stayed with us. We located a failing component card about an hour after the specialist arrived. At that point, we encountered another problem. Our parts room did not have the needed circuit card in stock. The parts folks did locate one down in Akron and they had dispatched a courier to get it. Since the customer was well south of the city, the courier would deliver the card directly to us to save time.

It was well past super time as we waited. Skip offered to go out and get burgers at a tavern just down the road. We offered to pay, but he would not hear of it. He said payment would be getting his machine running. The new card arrived as we were finishing the last of the burgers and fries. We quickly made the repair and began testing the operation. During this whole time, we had been standing as there were no chairs anywhere near the machine. Skip was tired (and bored), so had decided to rest by sort of sitting on the rim of a large metal wastebasket (if you can picture that). When I finally declared the machine up and running, Skip tried to stand up. Instead, his foot slipped and he came down in the wastebasket. After helping him to his feet and out of the basket, we all had a good laugh. Skip locked the place up and we headed down the road to that nearby pub for a celebratory beverage.

Still More Data

Another history pause. Currently, in the age on laptops and tablets, we expect all of a computer's components to be located on one "board," most often called the mother board. This was not always so. In the old mainframe computers, components were arranged on smaller "circuit cards." The cards varied in size from about 3" x 5" in early computers to foot wide cards in later models. One end of each circuit card contained a row of contact tabs. These cards were then plugged into larger boards containing row after row of sockets. This is where the term "motherboard" was really born. The backs of these socket boards were a maze of pins sticking out like rows of solders at attention. Interconnections were made by wrapping thin wires tightly around those pins. Usually, several of the motherboards (socket boards) were attached to a steel framework known as a gate.

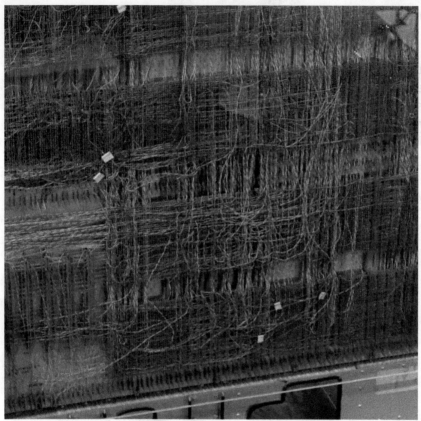

Pin side of a motherboard. Courtesy National Electronics Museum

Remember that those big mainframe computers used technology from 50 or 60 years ago. The IBM 1400 series computer from the early 1960s was the first to utilize transistors exclusively. All the 1400 System circuit cards were individual or discrete components, including transistors, resistors, and capacitors. The components were soldered onto the removable circuit cards which were then plugged into the motherboards.

The System/360, introduced in 1964, was the first to use integrated circuits which contained multiple components all in one housing. The integrated circuits were also mounted on removable circuit cards. As technology advanced, integrated circuits (now called "chips") included more and more components. Today's chips often contain more components than an entire 1400 System computer. Let that sink in for a moment.

Memories

Until the late 1960s, computer memory technology was such that a computer's memory was made up of thousands of tiny donut-shaped magnets. These magnets were so small that you could place several dozen of them on your thumbnail. This was "magnetic core memory" which was often shortened to just "core memory." The tiny iron cores were magnetized in one direction or the other to represent

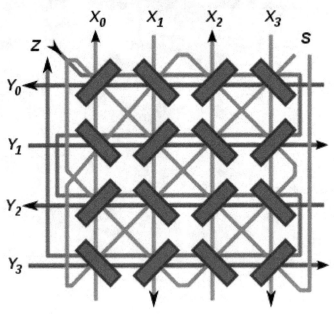

zeroes and ones. A group of eight tiny donuts was necessary to represent one character in the computer memory. All the donuts were strung together in a matrix by very thin insulated wires that ran through the donut holes. The wires made it possible to choose, or "address" the donuts in groups of eight. A very complicated setup, but it worked well until monolithic or "solid-state" memories were developed in the late 1960s.

The new solid-state memories were built into integrated circuits which were considerably faster and required far less power. Solid-state memories, as well as dual processing capabilities were first introduced in the System/370 in 1970. This monolithic memory technology remains today in all current electronic devices, albeit in a much reduced size.

Consider for a moment the physical size difference between magnetic core memory and solid-state memory. Despite the tiny size of core memory magnets, the matrix, the structure of a memory unit was about 6" square and about 12" high. The entire structure gave you a grand total 64K of memory. Because computers use a binary mathematical scheme, "64K" actually represents 65,536 "bytes" or characters of memory. That size was only for the basic unit containing the donut magnets and selection wires. In addition, power supplies, cooling fans, control circuitry and connections were needed. Today, even the smallest of smart phones contain "4Meg" (4,194,304 characters) of memory. Moore's Law endures more than 60 years later.

One more thing. Due to weight considerations, the necessary power supplies for core memory were always located at the bottom of each computer frame. Computer power supplies consumed huge amounts of power. So much that if a computer were to be suddenly powered up, the sudden power surge would trip circuit breakers and make the electric companies cringe. To alleviate that problem, computers were designed to turn on their power supplies sequentially.

Got a hammer?

The first mainframe computer on which I was in-depth trained was the System/360, model 40. Shortly after the completion of that training, we installed a 360/40 at Cleveland State University. CSU was a new state college based at the former Fenn College of Engineering and became the first urban university in Ohio. It was assigned to me. You might say CSU and I grew into mainframe computers together.

The memory on System/360 computers was the time-tested, but expensive core memory. At the time, a basic 64k memory unit cost roughly $64,000 (in 1965 dollars). That was a bargain, as this was the first computer memory to reach the "buck-a-byte" cost barrier. The high cost was due to the fact that the core matrix was completely handmade. Technicians at the plant actually strung the little magnetic donuts or beads by hand in an environmental clean room. The last step in the assembly process was to spray the whole unit in a very thin varnish to fix all the cores in position. This step was difficult and far from foolproof. Yet it was necessary due to the constant reversing on the magnetic polarity. The zeros and ones. The electric current going through the core tended to twist the donut. If not stabilized, the donut would rotate and wear the insulation off the wires strung within. The resulting short circuit was not a good thing.

The CSU computer was configured with the maximum 256k of memory. Therefore it contained four of the 64k memory matrix units. Two of the memory units resided in an add-on frame known as the 'H' frame. This was necessary due to additional power supplies for the memory.

On one occasion, the system developed a main memory error. Troubleshooting procedures were followed to eliminate voltage problems, loose connectors and bad circuit cards. The error was one bit of the eight necessary for one byte (character) of data. Just one of 65,535 donuts was bad. Due to the high cost of replacing the entire unit, I was required to call in the office memory specialist to verify the diagnosis.

Tommy arrived quickly and proceeded to the same conclusion. We disassembled the memory matrix unit from all the connectors, power supplies, etc. in anticipation of replacing that component. With the basic core unit now on my workbench, Tommy said, "I want to try one last thing before we replace the unit." Then he explained that sometimes, when a single donut comes loose and wears through the insulation, it is possible to eliminate the short circuit by moving the core a little to where the insulation is still good. Tommy looked around the bench and then asked, "You got a hammer around here?"

We put an ohmmeter across the wires that indicated a short circuit. I handed Tommy my hammer and he immediately beat on the top of the matrix frame several times. Checking the meter, we saw no change. He inverted the unit and again beat it vigorously. Success! The short circuit was gone. He picked up the unit and shook it about then tapped the unit on the bench from all sides. The short did not return. "OK, let's try it." After reassembly and reinstalling the unit, we ran all the memory diagnostics. They ran perfectly. That system remained free of memory errors until it was replaced by a larger System/370 model some years later.

I think I found it

In addition to fixing machines, CEs also installed many Engineering Changes (ECs for short). These were updates to the machine hardware, software or documentation. Often an EC included all three at once. Most ECs were fixes for some rare intermittent problem or an operational improvement. Occasionally circuitry was added for additional features. Most often ECs were the result of feedback to the manufacturing facility by CEs in the field. Engineering Change installations were normally designed to take less than a couple hours. For longer installations, it was necessary to schedule time at night or on weekends to minimize customer impact. On rare occasions, an Engineering Change might require many hours and multiple shifts. Fortunately for all concerned, they seldom required more than four to six hours.

Soon after its announcement in 1970, a System/370 model 145 was installed in our local Data Center. It was a show piece of "the latest and greatest" in computer hardware. The new system was fully compatible with the previous System/360, so prospective customers could try out the new technology with their current programs and data. A full round the clock schedule of demonstrations and customer trials meant that any Engineering Changes had to be scheduled for a Sunday.

One Sunday morning in the fall of 1970, Bob and I tackled an engineering change on the Data Center's 370/145. It involved about four hours of rewiring the pins on the back panels of several motherboards. Several circuit cards were changed and new cards added.

ECs always included a very detailed set of instructions. The first section of the instruction sheets listed each wire that was to be removed. This was followed by a section listing the new wire connections to be made. Last was the section that changed circuit cards and other miscellaneous items.

97

For safety reasons, as well as quality control, CEs always installed changes in teams. On this occasion Bob read each instruction while I performed the actual operation. We utilized specialized tools to unwrap old wires from the back panel pins and another tool to wrap new wires where needed. When all steps were completed, we switched roles so that I did the reading and Bob verified my work. I read the location of one end of a wire and Bob told me where it went. Mistakes were simply not an option.

After all steps were completed and verified, it was time to power up the system and run tests to prove that all went well. Bob remained near the area in which we had worked. I moved around to the opposite side of the machine to reset all the circuit breakers. With that accomplished, the power-on switch was pressed to begin sequencing the power supplies. Each step of the sequence resulted in the audible click of a relay followed by the humming of a power supply. Suddenly, a loud bang and silence. Special circuits had sensed that something was not right and killed all power instantly. That circuitry was known as a "crowbar" since it brutally yanks down all power supplies to prevent further damage to the machine. And yes, one of the circuit breakers was tripped.

Bob and I agreed that somewhere, somehow, we must have made a mistake. Once again, we rechecked every step of the change. After going through the entire set of instructions, again we found no errors. Something else was going on in there.

The next troubleshooting step involved a special feature available only in "CE mode" that allowed us to manually turn on each power supply in the correct sequence but without the automatic crowbar circuits being active. This way, we could check each power supply to ensure the correct voltages were being produced.

Slowly, we began the procedure. Upon arrival at the step containing our suspect power supply, it powered up successfully and voltages were within tolerances. However, from the opposite side of the machine, Bob yelled out, "I think I found it!" With that, I stood upright to see Bob standing across the machine from me. There was a thin plume of white smoke rising in front of his face. Indeed he had found the problem.

It was easy to find the burnt wire that indicated a short circuit. We removed the crispy critter and set about finding the cause. We determined the cause to be a typographical error in the instructions. A wrong pin number had caused a power supply wire to be connected directly to a grounded pin. Not good. We quickly found the errant instruction, but now the problem was where did the errant wire really belong?

Every Engineering Change included updated pages for our logic diagrams. We began searching through the new logic pages and soon found ourselves tracing wires with very unfamiliar names. We decided the strange circuit names had to be for some newly added circuit or a feature not yet announced. From the names and associated circuits, we had a pretty good idea what the circuitry did. Soon we found the correct wire location and applied a wire to the proper pin.

As soon as we had everything working again, we phoned the plant site where the Engineering Change had originated. Fortunately every plant location had at least one engineer available at all times for emergencies. The Plant Engineer immediately initiated a warning and correction so that no one else would be faced with this problem. In other words, the Field Engineering cycle begun by Hollerith still worked.

It's not really there

Every computer has a limited amount of physical memory to be utilized by programs and data. That means there is a limit as to how much work a computer can do at one time. The control program or operating system is therefore limited by this physical restraint. Everyone who worked with computers knew that.

That scenario all changed when the System/370 and its new computer operating system program called Operating System/Virtual System1 was introduced. OS/VS1 included something called Virtual Memory. The concept of virtual memory is complicated, but through a combination of special hardware circuits and the new OS, each and every program could be made to think it had all the memory it needed. Each program thought it was the only one running on the computer. The concept was further improved with OS/MVS, which allowed multiple instances of virtual memory. That sounds like magic, so how did they do it?

Remember that computers run at speeds measured in nanoseconds and mainframe computers were already capable of "time-slicing" multiple programs at the same time. The multiple program juggling act was possible due to something called an "interrupt." Each program "interrupts" the mainframe when it needed some particular function. The operating system prioritizes the various interrupts so that the mainframe was still doing only one thing at a time. Just really, really fast. The interrupt scheme enabled a more efficient use of the computer's circuits.

This new OS/MVS did that but also kept track of where each program resided in the computer's memory, how much space it was using and how often it requested an interrupt. Slower running programs could now be temporarily moved out of the computer's physical memory space and into a special reserved area of disk storage. This occurred very quickly using the special hardware circuits. Just as quickly the program could be moved back into the computer's memory when necessary.

How about a very simplified example of how a virtual memory system works? This explanation will take a minute, but remember the speed at which a computer is actually running.

Let's say one program is waiting for a line of characters to finish printing. As computer speeds go, printers are very slow. The Operating System notices this program is waiting for something. So, rather than have it take up valuable memory space, the O/S calls on the special hardware controls to move the waiting program out to the virtual storage area. Other programs now have more real memory to use. The O/S is still keeping track of that program now residing in Virtual Memory. When the printer eventually signals (interrupts) that it has finished its task, the O/S tells the hardware to move the program back into real computer memory so the next instruction can be executed.

OK, if you knew all that, it was probably boring. On the other hand the reader may still be totally lost. Sorry if you experienced either outcome, but I thought that an explanation might help to fully appreciate the next episode. By the way, this is really a continuation of the previous story involving that "smoke test" during the Engineering Change installation.

Too Late

"Nothing is done until the paperwork is finished." The last step of any Engineering Change was always to update the logic diagrams so they reflect the changes just made. Every machine included hundreds of pages of Logic diagrams. This was necessary due to the thousands of electronic circuits in a computer frame. Each loose leaf type page was huge by book standards. The pages measured about 12" x 18" and it took many volumes to contain them all. Anyway, Bob and I completed the EC, including the updating of our logic books. We cleaned up the area and headed home.

Monday morning around 10AM, my manager Don called and asked if we had EC number such and such for the 370/145. I told him we had installed it the day before. Now excited, he said, "I just got a call and you are not supposed to install that EC. There are major problems with it." I explained that we knew of the problem and, in fact, Bob and I were the ones who sounded the alarm. Furthermore, we corrected the mistake and all was well. Now calmed down, he said "OK" and that was that.

Less than an hour later, Don burst into our CE room all excited again. "Where is the paperwork from that EC?" I told him it had been filed as always. He said, "I need everything that came with that change!" I retrieved the instruction package from our file. He added, "I need the logic pages too." I said, "Sorry Don, they are already filed." "Damn. I was told to immediately return EVERYTHING." Well that could not be done because after filing the new logics, the old ones were destroyed to avoid any confusion. With that, I realized the problem. Besides the instruction typo error, they had sent the logic pages containing information on the unannounced Virtual Memory feature. That was the feature we found while trying to correct the EC error.

I yanked the boss's chain a bit. I said, "Gee Don, we aren't supposed to know about virtual memory?" I thought he would explode. "Don't you EVER say one word about that to ANYBODY!" Neither Bob nor I said another word about it. At least not until after the announcement the following year.

101

Private Flight

This is another story involving an Engineering Change, but far different from the last one. For a fairly long time, I was assigned the Blue Cross Blue Shield account in town. I had scheduled a rather long EC for a Saturday. The change went well and in no time at all the mainframe was back up and we were running tests to ensure everything functioned properly. Near the end of the test, there was an error code generated. I restarted the tests while I investigated the code. My diagnosis pointed to one of the circuit cards added in the EC. The second test run verified the error by generating the exact same code. A call to our parts room soon confirmed my fears. The brand new card was not yet in stock. They checked the parts system and found that the new cards had not been added to any parts center anywhere in the country.

We called the plant of origin. The engineer on duty confirmed that there were delays in getting the new cards into distribution. He was aware of the critical nature of my problem and agreed to go down to the factory floor and pull the required card from manufacturing stock. He called back in half an hour to let me know he had the card and had already called one of the pilots they had available for such emergencies. He was about to leave for a local airport to meet the pilot. An hour later, he called again to give me the pilot's name, his destination, ETA and the Cessna's tail number. For reference, the tail number is a unique number assigned to each and every aircraft by the Federal Aviation Administration.

The Blue Cross Data Center Manager had been informed of our problem and had arrived on site. He was thoroughly impressed by the lengths to which we went to get his machine working again. He bought coffee and we talked until it was time to head out to the airport. As soon as I said it was time for me to go, he asked to go along and then insisted on driving. We drove to the county airport about 10 miles away. We walked out onto the tarmac and found a bench just outside the door. A small plane landed within minutes of the ETA I was given. Sure enough, the tail number matched. The Cessna taxied over near us and killed the engine. The pilot got out carrying a small box. After brief hellos and goodbyes, the pilot headed back so he could be home before dark. That did indeed fix the error code and we had a very happy customer despite being down hours beyond the scheduled time.

The Junk Yard

Earlier I told of a school experience involving the 7772 Audio Response Unit. That school actually occurred well after this incident. In 1974, I was assigned a similar unit at National City Bank of Cleveland. Actually mine was a 7770 ARU, which was like the 7772 but differing in the means used to generate the audio responses. Fortunately for me, the machine sat quietly for years along one wall of the computer room doing its thing. Until...

On a Friday evening I got a call that the Audio Response Unit was not responding to inquiries. I drove to the account knowing nothing except that the machine logic books were located near the machine itself. On arrival, the management staff was upset because their branch offices could not make inquiries and it was needed especially through the weekend.

I opened the covers to find cooling fans whirling away and power seemingly OK. On one side, at the upper left corner of the machine I located a drum shaped component. It reminded me of pictures I had seen of the old Edison recording cylinders, but larger and it was the color of iron oxide. Surrounding it were rows of small objects that looked much like tape recorder read heads. I surmised that the audio responses were recorded on that drum. However, the drum was not turning.

The immediate question was what makes the drum turn and most important, when should it be turning. Turning to the logic diagrams revealed that there were 132 words recorded on the drum and the drum should be in constant motion. A computer program selected which words to read and in what order. The machine made that happen. In checking the drum assembly, I found that the drum shaft was free to turn so the bearings were not bound up. Also, the correct voltage was present at the motor terminals. It should be running! Obviously a bad motor.

The part number for a new motor was found and I called our parts room. Their response was, "We don't stock that part. It has been discontinued and referred to the plant." I dug around and found that the plant in Raleigh, NC was responsible for Audio Response Units. (As long as any machine exists in the field, a plant site is designated as responsible for it.) More digging found a phone number. The engineer on the other end checked and determined there were no 7770 drum motors anywhere in the country. He said our only hope was the junk yard.

Actually this junk yard is not as bad as it sounds. These were just areas in a warehouse where a batch of used machines were stored for at least 10 years after manufacturing ends. Just in case. This was one of those times.

The plant called back in less than an hour to tell me he had extracted a drum unit from one of the machines. He said he could remove the motor and send it. However, he recommended I take the entire unit just to be sure there was not another cause for the nonfunctioning motor. I agreed. He packed it for air shipment on the next flight which would arrive early Saturday morning. It was time for a few hours sleep.

Early the next morning, I picked up the box at the airport and headed back to NCB. Although coming from a junk yard, the replacement unit was far cleaner than our old one. All that was necessary was for me to exchange the two components and make the connections. The computer operator found the vocabulary load program. This program would write the previously selected words onto the magnetic coating of the drum in the same manner as a tape recorder. She ran the program and we were back in business. Although it took a long time, it was an easy fix. And that is how we learned about the existence of computer junk yards.

Bowling Night

In the "good olde days" CEs did much socializing after work. One fun activity was the bowling league. We had enough people willing to spend one night a week out with coworkers to field eight teams, so we had our own league. Due to the nature of our work, each team had an alternate and we even allowed play with one man short using the missing bowler's average. It was simply a fun thing. At times the competition was fierce, but always good natured.

104

We bowled just a block from our office at a second floor bowling alley. It was located above what was once an American Harvester Truck dealership. The long stairway carrying your bowling ball was an endurance test in itself. The league started at 6:30PM, so there was ample time to catch a bite of supper before the games began.

Since the bowling alley did not serve adult beverages, it was customary to continue discussions at the hotel lounge next door to our office. At one such session, while we were enjoying lively conversation with brown bottles in hand, one of our dispatchers burst into the room. Ron still had his telephone headset on as he frantically looked around the room. Finally he spotted us and hastily headed our way. He apologized, but said that the Bobbie Brooks system was down and he could not find us. Us was Bob and me. At the time, we were the only two trained on that particular mainframe. Ron had called my house only to be reminded that it was bowling night. He got the same response from Bob's wife. He ventured next door because where else would we be? Bob had left shortly before, so it was left to me.

With the office and parking right next door it took little time to go the four blocks to the customer site. It turned out to be an easy fix. Diagnostics located a bad memory card. In a half hour I had obtained a replacement, installed it and was running a diagnostic to verify the fix.

Then it was back to the bowlers. It had been less than an hour since I had left, so I was sure they would still be at the lounge. My chair was still empty. Before I could summon a waitress, the guy across from me pushed a beer across the table and said, "Here! You're one behind." No choice but to oblige.

105

13 - Suggestions

Many companies have established suggestion plans for their employees. So companies took them more seriously than others, but none was completely altruistic. At the heart of the program was the bottom line. Sometimes an unnoticed detail or change in process can make a huge difference in the company product or service.

In our case, a special department was created in Endicott, NY to independently assess the value of employee suggestions. Ideas that proved to save the company money earned the employee a percentage of the first year's savings. A year later, each winning suggestion was automatically re-evaluated to determine exactly how much was saved. If savings were greater than the initially estimated amount, the employee was awarded an additional sum. There was no limit set. Likewise, there were minimum awards for safety or procedural improvements where real dollar amounts were small or could not be determined.

Cooling fan

Early on, three of us were engaged in installing an engineering change on some 2311 Disk Drives. These were the first disk drives made for the System 360. They were about the size of a dish washer. The machine's electronics were located on a single motherboard perhaps 12" x 15" high and shielded in a metal enclosure. The bottom of the enclosure was left open. At the top was a small cooling fan. The Engineering Change (EC) we were installing involved removing the fan assembly. It seems that someone had suggested eliminating the fan to save money. Supposedly the amount of heat generated at that point did not warrant power cooling. Convection currents would do the job since the top and bottom were otherwise open.

Gerry, Joe and I were talking about the change as we went about our business. Basically, we thought it foolish since we did not believe simple convection cooling would dissipate enough heat. The heat might cause early failure of the electronic components. Suddenly, Joe said, "We should write a suggestion to put the fans back on." Gerry and I laughed saying they would never accept the suggestion. They just went through the expense of removing the fans. The idea must have been verified before creating the EC. Joe decided to write it up anyway. Six months later, Joe was awarded over $3,000 for his idea. There really was a higher than expected rate of failure once the fans were removed. It was our own fault, but Joe did buy coffee as consolation. It was an early lesson that paid off later.

Of Personal Interest

Almost every CE wrote at least one suggestion during their careers. Most wrote dozens. Some wrote hundreds. This CE wrote his share. Perhaps more than his share. As expected, the vast majority of our suggestions were rejected.

Most of the suggestions that were accepted earned small or minimal awards but a few netted bankable awards too. Of the many suggestions submitted, a few experiences with the suggestion program stand out. Especially those ideas that were not winners.

Video Technology

Video technology back in the 1960s was primitive to say the least. Despite that, IBM engineers managed to mass produce the first video terminal system. It consisted of the 2848 Display Control Unit and 2260 Video Display Terminals. Although optional, almost all 2260 video terminals included a keyboard. The keyboard technology was borrowed from electric typewriters. The display itself was a digital raster device which contained only the vacuum tube circuitry to support the CRT screen. In effect it was a TV set without a tuner.

Raster technology refers to the controlled movement of an electron beam across the face of a Cathode Ray Tube (CRT) in successive lines moving down to the bottom. Then, reaching the bottom, the electron beam was quickly returned to the top. This was repeated over and over just like in the old pre-digital TV sets. When characters were to be displayed, tiny dots were added to the raster in an appropriate pattern. The reader might compare this with the way characters are formed on today's personal computer printers.

The data to be displayed on the terminal screen was actually generated and stored in the 2848 Control Unit. When a character was to be displayed, a character generator created the appropriate pattern of dots and stored them in something called an acoustic delay line.

The simplest way to explain how the delay line works is this: Imagine a piece of stiff wire, like piano wire. If you twisted one end, that tweak would move down the wire to the other end. If someone else were holding the other end, they would feel the movement. In this case, the wire was coiled around and around the same way a tape measure is coiled in its housing. The delay line was adjusted to exactly the length of time it took for one scan of the display raster. To display a dot pattern on the screen, all that was necessary was to tweak the wire at the correct times.

Dot spacing

So, on to this great idea. One day while troubleshooting a problem in a 2848 Control Unit, Gerry and I noticed a wire in our logic diagrams labeled "character spacing." Neither of us had noticed it before. After solving the initial problem, we decided to investigate that mysterious line further. It turned out that the line controlled a "variable character spacing" feature in the 2260 Displays. We also found the adjustment for the feature amongst the vacuum tubes on the 2260's common circuit board. Due to other factors, only the Model 1 (of three available models) was capable of utilizing the feature. The Model 1 was also the smallest and by far the least popular of the three 2260 models.

We managed to locate a Model 1 on which we could experiment. In moving the adjustment we could barely see any difference on the display. Moving the adjustment from one extreme to the other resulted in only the slightest difference in the space between the displayed characters. Digging deeper we found some documentation that stated that the adjustment could make a difference of "1.5-3.0 dot diameters." It was no wonder it was barely noticeable.

The 2260s all used a common circuit board, so all of these displays included all the required circuitry even though only a small fraction of them were capable of using the feature. We smelled big bucks in a suggestion to eliminate the feature. We found we could eliminate 5 components from every 2260 circuit board. Each 2260 was connected to the control unit by a 20-some wire cable, of which one

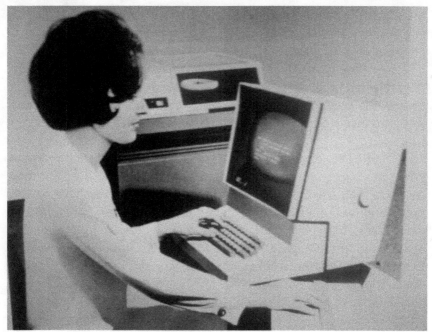
2260 Display Terminal, Model 1

was dedicated to this function. And, each 2848 control unit contained 3 circuit cards to support the feature. We carefully co-wrote a suggestion defining the issue and describing exactly how to eliminate the unnecessary feature and its components.

Our answer came back. Denied. The reason given was the 2260/2848 Display System could not be altered because the feature we proposed eliminating was already "printed in the sales manual." We agreed that was not an acceptable answer. Especially not since our research indicated that 95% of the displays could not even use the feature. We began surveying our customers, both the operators and management to determine how aware they were of the "Variable Character Spacing Feature." The universal answer: "huh?" Next we asked several IBM salesmen what they knew of the feature. Same response.

With that ammunition, we re-submitted our suggestion including a challenge to find 2260 operators who were aware of the feature, even internally within the company. We also reiterated the savings to be gained and gave estimates of the saving on each 2260 and 2848. There was no response for 3 months. We sent an inquiry as to the suggestion status. About 30 days later we got a response: "Under evaluation." There were several more delays. Finally, a year and a half after our original suggestion, the re-evaluation was complete. Basically it said yes you guys are right, we could save money, however "due to the projected product life and based on new products to be introduced shortly, the suggestion is denied." The replacement, the 3270 System was introduced in 1971.

We had uncovered a major flaw in the suggestion system. When the Suggestion Dept. evaluators ran into any technical question, they are not equipped to make a judgment. In such cases, the suggestion was forwarded to someone with knowledge in that area. In most cases, that meant the folks that either designed the product originally or those now responsible for it. Too often judgments were then made for reasons other than improving the product or reducing costs. Sometimes the dragon won.

Background

Companies continually update their products, introducing new machines with more speed, capacity or whatever. Sometimes a machine that performed well was utilized in systems other than the one it was originally designed to support. An example of this was the 1403 Line Printer. It was introduced with the 1400 System in 1959. Production continued through the System 360 and System 370 series systems into the 1980s.

Another such a product was the 2314 Disk Storage System. This was IBM's first multi-disk storage subsystem. It was composed of a control unit and 2 disk drive configurations. The 2312 contained one disk drive while the 2313 contained two drives. Each Disk Subsystem could be configured with up to nine disk drives. Eight of those drives could be operated at the same time with the 9th being designated a spare. Data was stored on "disk packs" that looked similar to very large chocolate cakes with clear plastic covers and they were all removable.

The subsystem was designed with an ID plug to uniquely identify each of the disk drives. Any disk drive could be any specific address by simply changing the ID plug. If a problem was encountered, the operator simply moved the disk pack to the spare drive, along with its identifying plug. He would be back up and running in a minute or two.

The 2314 Disk System was also the last disk drive to use a hydraulically powered mechanical access mechanism to position the read/write heads. Because the data disk packs could be moved between different drives and the mechanics involved, adjustment of the access mechanism was required to ensure interchangeability of the disk packs. The spare drive also allowed a CE to make his adjustments without impacting customer operation.

The alignment process involved a special CE Disk Pack and the use of an oscilloscope to visualize the data from the disk. This CE Pack was specially written with the middle track, number 50 missing. Tracks 49 and 51 were purposely written in ovals rather than perfectly round. The two ovals were also written 90 degrees out of phase. When track 50 was viewed on an oscilloscope, the resulting image was that of two lobes that looked like cat-eyes. Adjustments were made to ensure the "cat-eyes" were of equal size. That ensured that the missing track 50 was located exactly half way between the two oval tracks. Ingenious and it provided an extremely accurate adjustment.

But… Each one of the read-write heads had to be adjusted individually. To do this, the CE had to individually select the head he would be adjusting. That was accomplished by using two short jumper wires on the back panel of the disk drive's motherboard. If you recall, the back of these motherboards were a maze on pins and wires. Unfortunately one of the two pins necessary to select a given read head was located just one pin removed from a grounded pin. An errant jumper would cause a short circuit, which in turn caused the entire machine to power off. That fact resulted in much CE perspiration and an occasional dead machine. More than one customer forbad CEs from doing any alignment except in the wee hours.

No switch for you

A light bulb went on one day that a switch of some kind might solve the problem. Adding a switch in each disk drive and wiring it to the appropriate pins was impractical. I finally settled on the idea of a connector that matched that of the back panel pins. Such a connector could be placed over the appropriate set of back panel pins and be wired to a switch box. That way it eliminated the possibility of a short circuit and could be used on any of the disk drives. I built a prototype of the tool and it worked as planned.

Next step was a formal suggestion. The forms were completed to include diagrams and instructions on how to build the tool. Also included was a photo of my prototype. In the meantime, word had spread around the office and I was getting requests to build more switch boxes. I convinced my manager to OK a small budget to purchase the necessary parts. Several more of the tools were built and placed in larger accounts around the city. A couple CEs even built their own switch boxes from the plans.

Finally, my suggestion answer came back. Not only denied, but with a list of half a dozen reasons: 1. We do not need it. (!?!?) 2. Too expensive, etc., etc. When they did not come back with one good logical reason, but a group of flimsy excuses, you just knew there was more to the story. They would not budge on their decision.

As time went on, we had been split into three working groups, those who worked with the "old gray iron," intermediate sized systems and mainframe systems. As a result, little attention was paid to the smaller systems. Approximately a year later, IBM announced a new mini-computer. It went unnoticed.

One day I happened to be in the Data Center. A fellow CE called me over to the new mini-system installed there for demonstrations. He pointed out that the front of the disk storage machines looked exactly like the 2314 disk drives but the machine type number was different. He took me around back and opened a machine cover. Pointing, he said, "Isn't that your switch box?" What a shock. There it was, in the lower right corner of the machine. A switch numbered exactly like my switch box. Documentation verified that it was, in fact, for the exact same purpose. They had used the suggestion, even though they "did not need it" and it was "too expensive," etc.

Immediately I filled out a suggestion form protesting the use of my idea even after it had been turned down. Several weeks later I received the answer. They did not feel an award was warranted since I had not specified that particular (then non-existent) machine type on my suggestion form. After all, this was an entirely different computer system.

My manager was the next stop. He agreed that this was indeed a dirty trick and vowed to dig into it. After months of trying, we gave it up. The dragon won again. However, my effort was not a total loss. At the next branch-wide office meeting, I was surprised with a handsome local award for my efforts.

Vampire cleaner

Late in my career, I found myself working in a banking account. In the banking business, the processing of checks was of the utmost importance. Back in 1973, IBM introduced the 3890 High Speed Document Processor. Processing meant reading a document, sending the data to a mainframe computer where it was recorded and analyzed, then sorted into 1 of 36 output pockets. This machine was also huge. With all its features, it measured over 40 feet long! This monster was amazingly hardy. Machine production finally ended in 2005, but many are still in use today.

One of the machine's many maintenance items was to check the air pressure at various locations in the machine. Pressure checks were also used as a troubleshooting technique. The 3890 contained yard upon yard of air hose throughout the machine. All the hoses were made of a clear self-sealing material about 5/16" outside diameter. So that actual operating pressures could be measured, a pressure gauge was attached to a small block which was hollowed out to fit halfway around the hose. Centered in the cutout was a small, sharp, hollow pin to penetrate the hose. When the tool was removed after use, the tiny hole would reseal itself and not cause any problems. For rather obvious reasons, CEs dubbed it the vampire tool.

The tiny hole within the tool's pin was bored off-center so that a hard steel pinpoint actually broke the tubing surface. The offset hole prevented any material from entering the tool as it was inserted. Still, as heat from the machine aged the tubing, it became slightly stiffer and a bit more brittle. Pieces of hose material still managed to become lodged in the tiny hole. The tool became unusable since the hole was so strategically placed and tiny that it could not be cleaned. There was no choice but to replace the tool... at a cost of approximately $150 each.

One day, while sitting in my dentist's chair suffering through a root canal, the light bulb suddenly glowed again. As part of the procedure, dentists use tiny tapered files to clean the canal. I asked my dentist what he did with the used files. He explained that they are single use due to hygienic concerns. They simply threw them away. I asked if I could have those he used on me. After explaining my idea, he willingly obliged and gave me the several sizes he had used. He added that were actually quite inexpensive and added a small unused packet. I experimented on an old clogged vampire tool and found the best size dental file to use. Fortunately the size in additional packet was the best choice. I distributed the spares to several other banking CEs. Naturally that was after I submitted a suggestion to make the dental files available as a vampire tool cleaner. This suggestion resulted in a nice four figure award. Amazingly even pain can inspire!

You never know

Every day was an opportunity for CEs. The engineering mind is always looking for a better way. Every CE experienced that sudden glow of an idea. A non-engineer friend of mine suggested that engineers are just lazy. We keep looking for the easy way out... but stumble onto better ways in the process. Regardless, the ideas did make for better products and procedures. And occasionally there was a little extra money in the pocket.

14 – Fun Times

Most of the time CEs were under the gun, so to speak. A down system was serious business to customers who depended on their expensive systems to operate their companies. Often systems broke down at inconvenient times. As we have seen, sometimes in weird places. On the other hand, mainframe problems were occasionally an opportunity for the enjoyment of life. There were fun times too.

As mentioned before, the very first mainframe (also called a Central Processing Unit), that I was trained to maintain was the System 360 model 40. That was in 1967. And as the name implies, the CPU is the true guts of a mainframe computer system. It is the circuitry where all the calculating and processing takes place. Upon returning from the school, I was assigned the newly created Cleveland State University. Basically, the campus did not yet exist. Temporarily, the school utilized buildings from the previous Fenn College of Engineering. The computer department occupied the back half of the bookstore building. The entrance was an unmarked door in an alley. CSU had a unique, intellectually stimulating atmosphere that was loaded with interesting people. It literally invited people-watching.

Hi, how's it going?

Back then (I say that a lot now days), the system 360/40 was used for all of the campus computing needs. That meant it did everything from payroll and accounting, to running research programs for several departments and even running programs for students in various programming classes. This was still the era where programs existed on decks of IBM cards. In fact, all input was from punched cards or commands typed on the system console. Disk drives were still too expensive to be used for other than temporary storage while processing data. Permanent storage was on 10" reels of tape and output was printed out on paper or punched into another deck of cards.

Programming course students were required to write their programs and punch the data into cards themselves. They would add an identifier card to the beginning of the card deck, bind it with a rubber band, than submit it at one of several pickup stations. One of the campus mailmen (usually a part-time employee/student) would

115

transport the card decks to the computer room. Student jobs were run when higher priority programs were finished. The output of a student job would be printed out and wrapped around the program card deck with the student ID card on top. The rubber band held it all together. The next mail round would return it to the student's drop point. This system kept the computer busy around the clock.

One morning, the computer operator ran into the CE room and said, "Quick! You gotta see this." I followed her back onto the computer room floor. She said, "Look at the console." The System 360 operator console was actually a special adaptation of a Selectric typewriter. Operators entered commands on the keyboard and the computer printed a log of commands, jobs runs and various other messages as necessary. The last line on the scrolled log read, "Hi how's it going?" Nothing more. It did not contain the usual beginning identification codes. Only those words.

The machine displayed no error indicators. The computer appeared to be absolutely normal, except it was not doing anything. It just sat there in a "wait state." All indications were that it was simply waiting for the operator to complete some task or waiting for the operator to start another job run. The operator demonstrated that if the printer was made ready, the paper just slowly advanced without printing anything. When she placed a deck of cards in the card reader, they just "flushed" through until the hopper was empty. She mounted a tape. The machine did its normal automatic loading routine and the ready light appeared. Immediately the light extinguished and the tape unloaded itself. It was like something out of a science fiction movie. "What are you doing Dave?" (2001: A Space Odyssey)

Finally, I said to the operator, "I wonder what would happen if you answered it?" Reluctantly, the operator typed in "Fine." With that, the console typed out "that's good" and all functions of the system returned to normal. The only alternative would have been to "take a core dump." That phrase was often abbreviated a bit. The core dump was a special program that would print the contents of the computer's entire memory. It resulted in a stack of paper a foot or more high. The "dump" was then handed over to Systems Programmers, who would analyze it to determine what caused the system to "hang." I told her that if it happened again, we would have no choice but to run the core dump program. This was always a last resort because everything in the computer was lost and current programs had to be rerun.

Fifteen minutes later the operator was back. "It did it again." The core dump was taken and the system was IPL'd (restarted). That acronym stood for "initial program load." There were no further incidents that day.

Several days later, I saw the CSU Data Center Manager and asked him if they ever solved the mystery. He said yes, that a student job had caused the problem. The student had actually hacked the computer's operating system. I asked if the student had been disciplined or expelled. He said, "Heck no. I hired him." My jaw dropped but he quickly added, "Better he's on our side."

In the "olde days", really smart people hacked computers just because they could. It was an ego trip proving how smart they were. They never did any damage, they were just showing off. By the way, even back then hackers came in both genders.

No pioneer

Sometime later, a huge building program resulted in new classroom buildings, a library, a student union and the signature CSU Tower. The computer department was now located on three floors of the tower. The computer room occupied only half of the middle floor. The other half was earmarked for expansion. The space however was not wasted as it was temporarily used for band and choral group practice. I was still assigned the account, but the Data Center Manager had moved on to another job.

His replacement, Jim, was extremely well qualified for the position. He was a somewhat reserved individual who always wore a suit, as opposed to his predecessor's more casual dress. We got along well and enjoyed an excellent rapport. As customer managers often did, Jim would occasionally ask our opinion before making a business decision. As he put it, CEs were another resource. Our sales people were also well aware of this.

Shortly after IBM had announced a new disk storage system, the salesman asked me to accompany him for his presentation meeting. He knew that I had already been trained on this disk system. At the appointed time, the salesman began his spiel pointing out all the advantages of the new product. He also pointed out that I was already trained so everything was in place except for CSU's order. He proceeded to inform the customer that IBM was looking hard for an educational institution such as CSU to be "first on the block" with these new machines. With that, Jim suddenly stood up and complete with an appropriate accent said, "Don't wanna be no pi-o-neer. Them's the guys with the arr-as in their backs." I'm pretty sure he could tell I was doing my best not to fall on the floor laughing. The sudden outburst was completely out of character for his normally reserved nature. The salesman got the message. A good year later CSU did upgrade to the new disks but only after there was abundant local experience with them.

Der Lederhosen

Very early one morning I was called in from home to fix a disk drive problem at CSU. When I arrived at the tenth floor of the CSU Tower, I was greeted by an operator I had not seen before. He was in full costume. I was not sure if it was German or Swiss. The lederhosen, loose fitting white shirt, suspenders, knee socks complete with tassels, the whole thing. He was very friendly and polite. Despite careful listening there was no hint of a Bavarian accent. As I went about my business, I noticed that during the times between readying computer jobs, he sat quietly at the console reading a book. When I finished, it was almost dawn. Too late to go home. I decided to work until around noon and then take off the rest of the day.

When the first shift people arrived, I asked the supervisor about this operator. He chuckled and told me he never knew what Daniel's costume of the day would be. He came as a Scot complete with kilt one day. Another day he might look to be fresh from the West Virginia hills. Maybe he would be Greek or Oriental on yet another day. He explained that Daniel was a bit eccentric, but the best damn operator he had ever seen. He requested to work nights so he could go to school during the day. Daniel was an honest to goodness professional student. He had been going to Case Western Reserve University for years. Currently he was exactly one course shy of three different degrees and working on a 4th. Takes all kinds.

The 360 Quick Reference Card

Back to school

Personally, I had never finished my college degree. In fact, I had completed only my freshman year before becoming a CE. Since I was at CSU almost every day, I decided to enroll in night classes to continue toward a degree. It was not easy since we were now a family of four, but my wife and youngsters were very supportive. I trudged on.

One evening after a math class, the professor motioned for me to come see him. He said, "You're that IBM guy aren't you?" I was a little embarrassed but admitted I was. He had seen me around the computer room. That is when I realized I was a walking billboard. A suit, although the tie was now gone. A pager on my hip and the giveaway – a pen and pencil filled IBM pocket protector in my shirt pocket, complete with the famous "green card" tucked behind it. This green card had nothing to do with immigration. It was the folding 360 Quick Reference Card carried by every mainframe CE and many programmers. The card was heavy card stock that fan-folded down to the size of an IBM card. It fit perfectly into a shirt pocket. Anyway, it was a give-away.

After that I was more careful. Not only did the tie come off but so did the pager, the pocket protector, the green card and I never wore a suit coat to class. I left a jacket in my car for cool days and an appropriately heavier coat for wintertime. All was good until a couple quarters down the road when I signed up for a COBOL programming class. That was the major programming language for business applications. On the first day, I walked into the classroom incognito and took a seat about one-third of the way back. Five minutes later the instructor walked in, placed his books on his desk and looked up at the class. "John! What the hell are you doing here?" The instructor was one of CSU's programmers, making a little extra money by teaching at night. Busted again.

* * * * *

Beyond the ivy-covered walls of academia laid even more people watching fun. Such enjoyment could be had most everywhere. Some came from within our own ranks. Some from the customer people we contacted daily.

Don't tell me, tell my boss

We had a number of characters within our CE ranks. It probably came with the job. One particularly outspoken CE in our office was often called "the politician." Actually, I mentioned him before. I'm referring to Sam, the CE who took the clandestine photos of the yellow worm cooling system. Sam provided much entertainment for most of us. He once commented on a newly arrived Field Manager, stating that his name was penciled in on the roster. That was because he would not be here long enough for ink to dry.

To be fair, the Field Manager job was often just a rung on the way up the management ladder. Also changes were often made in trying to match the manager to his team and their customers. I lost count of how many managers I worked for over the years. We had one new Field Manager named Russ who was always checking on his people to make sure they were on time for their appointments. That was really not a good idea. CEs simply did not appreciate being micro-managed.

While Russ was our manager, I was involved in a large scale feature upgrade at another CE's account. It would take 15-16 hours to install. Naturally, it was scheduled for the customer's off-hours during the weekend. The first shift consisted of Sam and another CE who would begin the upgrade on Saturday at 4PM. The second team included Frank, the account CE, and me. We would relieve them at midnight.

The two of us arrived about ten minutes before midnight. That gave us time to do our usual crossover so that we knew how the change was going, etc. We grabbed coffees and gathered around the system console. Actually, Sam was sitting on the console table. He started a discussion by saying that Russ would probably call at 11:58. Soon we all had picked a time and bet a coffee on the outcome.

At exactly midnight, a phone on the console rang. Without hesitation, Sam reached over, picked up the receiver and said, "The number you have reached is not a working CE." There was a v-e-r-y long pause. Then Sam said, "Yep, it's me Russ." Following that incident we noticed that Russ was not nearly as concerned about our punctuality.

CEs were frequently praised or damned depending mostly on a machine rather than any personal accomplishment or lack there of. We accepted either with a grain of salt. Sam saw things in a different light. When offered praise, he habitually answered, "Don't' tell me. I know I'm good. Tell my boss. He signs the paychecks."

Joe Alphabet

There was a small closely held women's clothing manufacturer in town. It is gone now, but in its day, a visit there was a real "trip." On one occasion, I was shocked to hear music coming from the PA system. Previously it had been a cacophony of pages. "Peter, this is Paul, call me." "Rebecca, David is waiting in the conference room." "Sandy call Saul." It had been just one continues message all day long. The corporate culture seemed to be that of a dysfunctional family. If you listened to the pages, it seemed everyone was trying to be in control. You call me. It was actually rather comical.

On the other hand, upon entering the computer room you were always treated to a joke. Joe ???-ski was the first shift computer room supervisor. Even though you could not spell or pronounce his name, he was obviously of Polish decent. Everyone knew him as Joe Alphabet. Every single day, he had a different Polish joke to tell. They were never demeaning, just funny. He erased any negativity you might have harbored on arrival.

Getting Out of Town

While working the Saturday schedule, I was once called on to fix a problem at Oberlin College. This is a small, old time liberal arts college located in the town that provided its name. Oberlin is located about 45 miles west and south of our home base in Cleveland. The resident CE was out of town at a school.

My map got me to town and local signs pointed me in the right direction. The dispatcher did not have an exact street address, just "the administration building." The campus was a cluster of stone buildings from the late 19th century. Most buildings had raised entrances that all looked very similar as I drove the one-way streets. Finally I choose the most likely building only to find the main entrance locked, but a small sign verified that it was in fact the administration building. I noted a smaller entrance off to the left at ground level. It was open. I decided a computer room was likely to be on the lower level. That turned out to be a good guess. I entered to find a somewhat cramped computer room. At the system console sat what looked like a leftover Hippy from Woodstock - wild unkempt hair, full beard, shorts, Henley and sandals. Despite his appearance, he was articulate and knowledgeable.

After completing the repair, I approached the hippy operator to ask the best way to get back to Cleveland. He thought for a moment and then slowly said, "Well, man... I'd don't know. Maybe you could go down to the stop sign amd hang a left. Go 2 blocks and hang another left. That'll be Main St, so just stomp on and do oh, maybe 50. When the cop stops you, you can ask him for directions." As I stood there stunned, he laughed and said, "Well, just the first part. Left, 2 blocks another left. That will street will take you out to the highway." You never know what to expect on a college campus.

Super Nerd

Service Bureau Corp. employed about a dozen programmers at its local facility. These guys were all good. One was a tall, skinny guy whose suit always looked as if he had slept in it. One day I saw him sitting in a chair, slouched almost to a laying position in front of one of the computer consoles. He was periodically clicking an old windup stopwatch. I casually wandered over and said, "What's up Gene?" He said, "Oh, I'm just timing my program. I want to see how long it takes to run." I asked, "How are you doing that?" Gene's reply: "Well I forced my program to run in upper memory and I know that light right there turns on when it's running." I said, "You know, Gene, it takes several milliseconds for that light bulb to turn on. The CPU is running at nanosecond speeds." Gene sat up, looked at me, then back at the console. It was that moment of recognition when you realize that what you are doing is not the smartest thing. He stood and walked away without a word.

I was told by one of the operators that the reason Gene's suit looked like he slept in it was in fact because he frequently slept in his office, curled up on the desktop. The office wasn't big enough for a couch or easy chair. The operator also said Gene's wife once called to ask if anyone had seen him, because he had not been home for 2 nights. Actually, Gene had flown to California 2 days before for a seminar. I truly believe that some people are too smart for their own good.

123

The NASA Install

Shortly after returning from Basic School, I got volunteered for a system installation at NASA. The "John H. Glenn Research Center at Lewis Field" facility is located along the western edge of Cleveland Hopkins International Airport. This facility dates back to WWII when it was known as the Lewis Flight Propulsion Laboratory and was run by the NACA, the National Advisory Committee for Aeronautics. Its original purpose was aircraft engine research and was conveniently located across the airfield from the 2.2 million square foot aircraft factory where General Motors built B-29 bombers. The NASA mission continues today as a space science research facility.

In early 1967, we were installing NASA's System 360 Model 67. It was one of the largest computers of the day. The installation involved over 20 different frames when you include the input and output machines. With work continuing around the clock, it took two teams of CEs almost a week to complete the job. Even so, it was not all hard labor. Most of the experienced CEs were former Navy, so during lunch and coffee breaks us rookies were included in a running game of Battleship. The ocean grids were crudely drawn on printer paper.

Since the computer room was located on the second floor, each machine frame had to be loaded into an elevator and delivered to its new air-conditioned home. All went well until we tried to move the 2870 Multiplexor Channel frame. The frame was slightly larger than the other frames resulting in it being a bit too long to fit the elevator. First the covers and hinges were removed to reduce the length a few inches. The frame now barely fit the elevator.

New problem: The elevator door sensors detected an obstruction. The doors refused to close. So, the elevator company was called and soon a technician arrived. He bypassed the sensor so the elevator would work without the doors being closed. Finally, the second floor button was pressed and the elevator promptly moved several inches... down. The machine frame was too heavy for the hydraulic mechanism. Safety stops caught it to prevent any further descent. The technician managed to get into the space below the elevator and slowly increased the pressure allowance. Obviously the danger was that increased pressure could blow out a gasket. Not a welcome thought. The technician slowly increased the pressure just enough to cause the elevator to rise VERY slowly to the second floor. Five minutes later, mission accomplished. Break time.

Sleepin' on the job

Computer systems were always locked away in secure, windowless rooms. They did not understand the concept of normal business hours. They tended to break down on their own schedule. And, as already mentioned, customers wanted to utilize every microsecond of computing time. CEs had to be available 24/7. There were frequent "call outs" as well as some crazy schedules and weekend work.

When the phone rang at 1:00AM, it was to relieve an account CE. He had been called out early the previous morning and then, just as he was about to end his day, the mainframe in his account decided to malfunction. I knew him to be a very competent CE, so this must have been a difficult problem to diagnose. Although I only had about an hour's sleep, I did my duty and accepted the call.

On arrival, I found logic diagram books scattered about, and an oscilloscope plugged in and turned on. Not good signs. He brought me up to date on the symptoms, what he had already investigated, etc. I sent him home. It did not take long before realizing the difficulty here and I requested the assistance of our office specialist.

Jack arrived on scene around 2:30AM. We had coffee while I briefed him on the problem. I had narrowed the problem area to one board about half way up a gate on the left side on the mainframe. We had the logic diagrams open on the operator console a few feet away. Since he was fresh and far more experienced, Jack traced the circuits on the diagrams, while I manned the oscilloscope and reported back the signal levels at each location he gave. I was what we called the "scope dope."

The location of the circuit board made it difficult to stand or kneel. So I used a stool with casters that we employed for just such situations. Sitting on the stool, I responded with the signal level as Jack called out pin locations. The locations came rapidly as he traced a particular wire. At times, there was a pause as he pondered the next move. At one point, I was suddenly aware of Jack laughing. He was laughing at me. It seems I was dozing off sitting there on the stool. He said I would begin to fall off the stool and then stiffen as I caught myself falling. Apparently I had done this several times before his laughing actually woke me up. Obviously it was time for more coffee before continuing. A rough night, but we got the system up and running.

Escort Service

The Hough Riots took place in Cleveland in 1966. There was much looting and burning that occurred very near industrial and manufacturing facilities. In the aftermath, many area businesses hired armed guards to protect their property. Richman Bros., the manufacturer and retailer of men's clothing, was located just down the street from the western end of Hough Ave. To protect employees, they moved all employee parking to within a fenced area behind the building and hired a fulltime security firm.

Whenever it was necessary to visit Richman's during off-hours, we were told to only park in the no parking zone immediately in front of the building. A guard was stationed to notice anyone arriving and ensure there was not a problem. He would stand guard as we made our way to the door. Upon leaving the building, the guard would verify which car was yours. We were then instructed to wait inside the building until the guard motioned for us to come out. With that, he would draw his weapon and carry it down along his side as he slowly walked out to the cars. When he was sure no one was lurking in the shadows, he motioned for us to come out. He remained nearby until we were safely on our way. That routine remained in place until Richman Bros. closed in 1992.

Ten – hut!

A much lighter security story involved Bowman Products, a local distributing company to which I was assigned in the 70s. Bowman had experienced several small break-ins and robberies despite having employed a security company. They had decided it was time for a change. Interviews were scheduled with several security organizations.

I happened to be at the account one summer day when the Data Center Manager called me into his office on the front side of the building saying, "You gotta see this." (There it is again) It seems one of the potential security companies had arrived. We saw 5 security guards standing at attention on the sidewalk below. Soon another man sporting Captains bars came from the building with a clipboard in hand. Commanding them "at ease," he went to each guard where he talked briefly pointing to the clipboard on occasion. He then stepped to the front and dismissed them. He stood casually as they dispersed in all directions. It looked like nothing more was happening so we returned to our chores.

On the next visit, I asked if he knew anything more about the security people. The manager related the rest of the story. The security company we saw was owned by a former Army MP Colonel. He hired only former military guards – MPs, APs or SPs. When Bowman called him to discuss a contract, he told them that before he would bid on the job, he would survey the premises and then submit his bid accordingly. We had witnessed the beginning of his inspection routine. Following that, his security company agreed to bid on the job only if several security issues they found where eliminated first. They had found breaks in fencing, unsecured doors, etc. that needed to be corrected.

A later visit found new guards and security procedures for entry. The more I thought about it, what a great strategy for the Colonel. Impress the hell out of the prospect, then have the company repair security loopholes so that his people had less to guard. It worked, he got the job.

Ex-Shrink

Once I was assigned the system at a paint manufacturer's headquarters. It was a modestly sized system located in a downtown office building. I immediately noticed that the operators and other computer room people seemed very formal and businesslike. There was none of the usual camaraderie or joking around. They did their jobs, but no one seemed to be enjoying it. Turned out they were all in fear of Ron, the Director of Data Processing.

When I first met Ron I thought him to be a reasonable individual. What I did not know was that Ron had, on a couple

127

occasions, walked into the department and fired someone on the spot in front of other employees. Normally in the business world, such a task would be handled by the employee's immediate supervisor and in the privacy of his office. The reason for the atmosphere was obvious.

I also had reason to speak with the programming staff occasionally and noticed a similar lack of joy. The staff was always properly dressed. No jeans or sandals. Men were cleanly shaven. Women were in proper business attire. There was one exception. Alan, one of the Systems Programmers, wore his hair a bit longer and sported a full, but nicely trimmed beard. Given a black hat, he could have been mistaken for a Rabbi. Alan was easy to work with and did not seem to be affected by the general attitude.

One Friday we received a memo on Director of Data Processing stationery saying he had scheduled a meeting of all IBM representatives in his office the following Tuesday at Noon. The formality and odd time made it seem more like an order. Larry, my manager at the time had also received the memo. We had no idea what it was about. Larry and I met the account salesman and the assigned Systems Engineer as the appointed time approached.

Ron's office was not at all large. In fact, one of the chairs had to be moved to allow the door to close. Ron began the meeting by standing up, pounding a fist on his desk and saying, "Why am I not getting monthly maintenance on my tape drives?" I spoke up and explained that since we recently installed a new generation of tape drives, monthly maintenance was no longer required. Maintenance was now scheduled based on actual usage. The salesman tried to interrupt, but Ron raised a hand to stop him. As soon as I finished, my manager immediately stated that he would look into the situation. At nearly the same time, the salesman said he would have the Systems Engineer review the tape error logs. The rest of the meeting was routine and not in the least memorable. Following that meeting, my encounters with Ron were quite amiable, even friendly.

Later I had occasion to discuss Ron with Alan, the rouge programmer. Alan explained that he had found out that the boss was originally a Psychologist. Ron's professional life had taken such a personal toll on him that he decided to leave his practice for the business world. His previous training had given him an understanding of human nature and people control, but at the same time, he respected people who were not easily intimidated. He was a very interesting person indeed.

Sohio

The Standard Oil Company of Ohio, better known as Sohio, was a major account in Cleveland until they merged with (and soon thereafter absorbed by) British Petroleum. The main office was in the building next door to where I cared for the Republic Steel Corp. systems. Sohio was quite a large account and had several CEs assigned to it.

As luck would have it, their System 370 model 145 decided to burp one morning while both of the senior members of the CE team were absent. The remaining CE had minimal training on the mainframe so he called for assistance. I walked next door and went up into the computer room.

As I neared the mainframe, there were perhaps a dozen people gathered tightly around the operator console. They were an assortment of operators, programmers and I don't know who all. I stood on tiptoes to see poor Andy trying to run diagnostics at the console. About this time, Kellie the computer room supervisor came up behind me and said, "What are you doing back here instead of helping Andy?" I said, "I couldn't get there through the crowd." She immediately started yelling, "Get the hell out of the way so the CEs can do their work." The crowd quickly dispersed.

Andy and I were able to solve the problem in less than an hour. We had lunch and then I headed back at Republic Steel. Shortly thereafter I got a call from my manager. He asked what had happened at Sohio. I told him about the problem and that we had it running again in an hour or so. He said, "Well, you need to go apologize to Kellie." I asked why. It seems one of that crowd had been some bigwig from the software side of the house. He had called their IBM salesman claiming I was being a smartass with Kellie. Of course the salesman got upset at the thought of trouble in his account and the thought that he might lose some future sales. Naturally he passed that information along to my manager. So here we were. We discussed the matter, but my manager said it would be best if I smooth things over with an apology anyway.

129

I trudged back to Kellie's office. She greeted me with, "What, back already?" I said, "Yep, I was told I had to apologize to you." "For what?" I explained what had transpired and we both had a good laugh and commiserated about what a bunch of burden carrying animals salesmen and programmers were.

Error compounded

Probably the biggest mess ever encountered was while assigned the National City Bank account. NCB had several systems at that time. One was an IBM System 370 model 158. IBM had just announced a new feature which placed control circuitry for disk drives directly into the mainframe. Previously, all control units had been connected by cables to the mainframe through circuits called "channels." This new feature, Integrated Storage Control, allowed much faster transfer of data between the computer memory and the disk storage units.

Systems already in customer locations could be upgraded to this feature. It was the largest upgrade ever attempted in the field. It involved replacement of motherboards, adding a whole "gate" of boards, adding power supplies, connecting all the new components and modifying many old circuits to work with the new feature. Each section of the upgrade had its own bill of materials and instructions. I had planned for 2 two-man teams to work 8 hour shifts. The first team would return to finish the work and do the final testing. I scheduled myself to work the 1st and last shift.

The upgrade was scheduled to begin at midnight Friday to give us all Saturday and Sunday to finish... just in case. Everything had to be completed and back to normal come Monday morning. Before anything could be done, the current machine was verified as to all existing features and engineering change levels. This was necessary to ensure the correct bills of materials were sent. On arrival the contents of each required checking to ensure it was complete and correct. All the necessary pieces had arrived by Tuesday that week, giving plenty of time to check them over.

All went well until very early Thursday morning when I was called out to assist at another account. We finally got that machine working by mid-afternoon. Lacking sleep, I went home early. Then, at about 3AM Friday I got another call. This time for a rather rare machine that I was one of only two CEs in our office who were trained. The other CE was already on site and needed help. After that repair, I headed to my account. It had been a merry-go-round and my manager could see the result. He told me to go home. He had arranged for one of the CEs I had scheduled for the 2nd shift to swap with me. My manager was also aware that I had not yet completed the preliminary checks. For that, he called in our office specialist to complete that task. I went home for some much needed sleep.

Come Saturday morning I arrived about 8AM to continue with the second shift portion of the upgrade. Work was progressing normally and was well ahead of schedule. I was relieved to say the least. By mid-afternoon we were ready to begin the power-up procedure and begin testing. The machine powered up perfectly. We began running diagnostic tests. The diagnostics failed almost immediately. There were multiple failures in the original circuitry as well as in the new feature.

We immediately returned to the checkout procedure. Because this was such a large project, there was a master plan, which listed the sequence in which to install the different bills of materials. In verifying that, I found one bill of materials that was the wrong number. Somehow the factory had shipped the wrong bill of materials and it had not been caught. The bill of materials they sent was meant for a slightly different model. It contained one wrong motherboard and had caused the mis-wiring of several other boards. We were able to have the plant fly the correct b/m out immediately. Meanwhile we had to reverse the errant wiring while we waited for the correct bill of materials to arrive. In all, it took until Monday morning to recover. We were a little late in returning the system to the customer, but now everybody could go home and crash. Sometimes the best of plans go awry.

16 – Temp Assignments

As with any large company, the majority of employees spent their entire careers at one location. But it was also true that moves were fairly common. There was a joke inside IBM that the letters really stood for "I've Been Moved." There are times, such as when an employee is ready for a promotion, but there are no openings at his particular office. Obviously a move is necessary to gain the promotion. CEs were constantly on the move, but not always in that sense. It was not uncommon to be off to a school or seminar 5 or 6 times a year. Sometimes a move was for a temporary assignment of some sort. I was fortunate enough to have had the opportunity for a number of temporary assignments.

All the Way to San Jose

My career differed from many CEs in that I had a total of 5 temporary assignments over the years. And strangely, they were all at the same location, San Jose, CA. You couldn't ask for a nicer locale. A person can really get used to a place after a while. San Jose became more like a vacation home.

The first assignment came in late 1975. I had just returned from an extended software school in Kingston, NY. There was barely enough time to unpack when the assignment was proposed. It was for a nine month assignment beginning January 1st to work on a yet to be announced printer product. The deal was that if I took the assignment, the company would fly me home once a month for a few days' visit. Alternately, they would pay to move my family to San Jose for the duration. I would be able to take a limited amount of household goods so that we could setup a temporary residence at the location. Also included was a per diem allowance to help cover the added expenses such as rent.

Considering the length of the assignment, we elected to move the whole family. Of course the boys had to leave their friends in the middle of a school year, right at the Christmas break. That part was difficult for them, but they knew it was only temporary. It was amazing how quickly they got into the new routine and made new friends at their San Jose school. For that we were thankful.

The move was further eased by the fact that we knew some people in San Jose who had previously transferred there from Cleveland. Their presence provided some semblance of familiarity in a distance place. Also, we were able to take advantage of not having the usual household chores to extensively explore the area and travel the western US. We all experienced (and came to more fully understand) the cultural differences that make our country such a great place to live. That was an education in itself.

Since the product I would be working on was still under wraps, all I was told was that it was an all-new system printer meant to replace the venerable 1403 Printer. I was also told that the assignment would begin with a 2-month training program. Upon return to the office, I would be expected to assist the office when the new printer began shipping to the field.

Out With the Old

The 1403 had been IBM's workhorse printer since 1959. Its longevity was testament to its quality and endurance. The 1403 had continued IBM's habit of creating machines using unusual techniques and technologies (like the gyrating ball of the Selectric typewriter). The 1403 was similarly complex. Its technology involved a "train" of print character slugs being pushed around an elongated oval track at high speed. Electronic sensors knew exactly where each character was

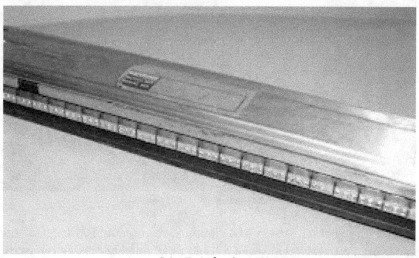

Print Train for the 1403 Printer

133

located as it spun horizontally around its track. And a very wide ribbon moved vertically across the speeding characters' path.

The 1403 used "fanfold" paper, where each page is attached to the next vertically. The left and right edges had ½" perforated tear strips that were used to smoothly advance the paper. The tear strips were discarded after printing.

Cover up revealing the paper path and mechanics.

The character train and ribbon were mounted in front of the paper on a moveable gate which could be opened to allow easy access to the paper supply. With the print train gate open, a box of paper was placed in front of the machine. The paper was then pulled up and into mechanisms called "tractors." Each tractor contained pins that matched the holes of the paper tear strip. These tractor mechanisms were capable of moving the paper extremely fast without tearing it! For that reason alone, all covers were required to be closed before the machine would print. No paper cuts here.

The paper passed over the top of the machine to be pulled down behind through a set of constantly running tension rollers. The paper was then re-folded into a stack at the rear.

In the center section of the printer, a row of 132 "hammers" resided behind the paper. At exactly the correct moment, a hammer would be electrically "fired" against the back of the paper. This forced the paper into the ribbon and into the intended character. Marvelously complex, but it worked.

For all its mechanical complexity, the 1403 Printer was capable of printing at 1,100 lines (not characters) per minute. However it was now being overshadowed by a new technology.

Fun with Printers

There was a 1403 program available that simply printed whatever was on a punched card. It created a printed list of the contents of any card deck. Such printouts were useful for many purposes including helping programmers de-bug their programs.

Somewhere along the line someone modified that program to print two cards on one line. All 132 print positions could be utilized. No one knows exactly where or when it started, but decks of cards began showing up that printed pictures on the 1403. Most were simple drawings or banners but there were also cartoon characters like Bugs Bunny and Elmer Fudd. However, some pictures were very sophisticated and detailed like a picture of the Mona Lisa.

The crazy complicated mechanism of the 1403 also made noise as the hammers forced the paper into the ribbon and character faces. It made a lot of noise. So much so that the inside of the printer covers included acoustic material to spare the operator's ears. Later, when the System 360 was introduced, another model 1403 was introduced that was fully enclosed. That finally reduced the noise to a reasonable level. Fact is the sound-deadening material was so extensive that this model included a motor to raise and lower the heavy cover.

A fully enclosed 1403 Model N1, retired in a warehouse.

The noises were not confined to the mechanics of the machine. The following is believed to have started at one of the plant sites when a technician brought in a portable radio to help pass the time. It was placed on top of a nearby printer control unit. When the radio turned on, there was much static. They noticed the static pitch changed as the data being printed changed.

This inspired some musically inclined programmer with too much time on his hands to create music from the static. Again, card decks appeared that caused portable radios to play a variety of tunes. There was even an excellent and very patriotic version of the Star Spangled Banner.

Later still, a program was written to allow the clattering printer to play music directly as it wasted paper. There were dozens of tunes. Even a rendition of "Raindrops Keep Falling On My Head."

Argonaut Project

Back to business. Xerox Corp. had been making copy machines using a technology they called Xerography. This multi-step process involved first creating a temporary electrostatic image on an intermediate medium. Then using a fine thermoplastic powder, called toner, the image was transferred to paper where the powder was fused (melted and pressed) onto the paper. Over the years, Xerox had improved the process considerably, but operational speed was limited by having to process one sheet of paper at a time. In the late '60s while trying to speed the process and improve print quality, they began experimenting with lasers.

IBM scientists also recognized the potential for laser printing. The major difference between Xerox and IBM was purpose. Xerox concentrated on single page copiers for the office. IBM was looking for a 1403 replacement. As such, any replacement would have to be faster, have better quality print and be as reliable as the old 1403. Thus began a project in 1969 that would use laser technology in the replacement printer.

Like most companies, IBM used code names for projects or products while they were under development. An official name and product number were never actually assigned until just before the product was ready to be announced and production begun. The future printer was dubbed "Argonaut."

Argonaut development proceeded through the early 70s and the decision to produce the machine was made in early 1975. It was destined to become the 3800 Printing Subsystem. This involved an entirely new concept in printing. As such, the company knew that CEs in the field would need to be totally retrained.

Argonaut became the 3800 Printing Subsystem. (The basic machine was 12 feet long.)

Before that could happen, there was a need for a core group of CEs with machine experience to install and maintain the early machines, as well as provide support for the newly trained CEs. That led to a small group of us from around the country being temporarily assigned to the San Jose plant site. During the 9 month assignment, we would learn everything about the machine from theory to assembly to troubleshooting. The first 2 months were planned as formal training using a couple of prototype machines.

Following the education phase, we would work in the Final Test Department alongside plant personal. Our job would be to help assemble the multiple frames for the first time, make the machines operational, then run a series of tests. After successful testing, we would disassemble the frames and pass them next door to the Shipping Dept. where they received covers and were packed for shipment. A few of the early machines were retained for long term testing.

Study break

Our course of study was detailed and thorough. Don, our instructor, was a Manufacturing Engineer turned teacher. He had been with the project all along and knew every detail. Don was a native of Los Angeles with an easy going yet dignified personality that somehow did not fit his mop of curly red hair in tight ringlets. His hair looked like a short red afro hairdo.

Half way through our studies, Don realized that we had already covered six weeks' worth of the material. The folks who created the course had seriously underestimated the skill levels, experience and absorption rate of CEs. Don took the time to discuss the situation with us. We could not finish early. The production schedule had been matched to our training. There would be no machines ready for us to work with. So, our routine had to change. First came hour long coffee breaks. Lunch became a 2 hour period, often away from the plant site. Finally daily class dismissal came an hour or more early. We slowed to a crawl but were still ahead of schedule.

You know how things can get a bit crazy when boredom sets in? One day, a CE from Georgia, unbeknownst to most of us, brought his newly completed radio controlled Sherman tank model to class. Whenever Don would turn to write on the white-board, there would be a low whirling sound and the tank would advance a little from behind the guy's chair near the back of the room. Don almost always stood to one side of the board so as not to cover anything he wrote. Soon the tank was in the center aisle and heading toward the front. About then, Don made a rare appearance at the center of the board. When he finally spotted the toy tank, a different pitch whirling sound accompanied the raising on the tank's canon. It was not that he registered any fear of the toy, but he discretely moved to the side anyway... just in case it was loaded. End of class. Play time.

A few days later, another CE arrived early with 2 shopping bags which he placed in back at either side of the room, out of the way. During breaks, our instructor often returned to his office for a few minutes to check for messages and return calls. During one such break, each of us was handed a Harpo Marx wig from the bags. We hid them under our tables. Later, while Don was writing on the board, a signal was given and all of us donned the wigs. When Don turned back toward the class, he was greeted by a room full of "mini-me's." He completely lost it. Class was over for the day.

After stretching our training to the assigned 8 weeks, we still did not have machines to work on. There had been some production delays due to last minute changes. During the lull we got to know the permanent final test crew quite well. There were also more long lunch breaks. We also spent considerable time playing with the prototype machines.

When production finally began, we helped assemble the frames according to an extremely detailed procedure manual. The procedures were in the form of a huge loose-leaf binder, about 6 inches thick! The instructions were unbelievably detailed. Each page went something like this:

13. Connect frame A, cable A031 to frame B, gate B, board A1, socket A03.
14. Measure the resistance between frame A, gate B, board B3, Socket H03, pin B06 and frame B, gate B, board A1, socket A03, pin B06.
15. Resistance should be <0.1 ohms.
16. Connect...

These detailed procedures served several purposes. First, factory employees were assemblers, not engineers. Most did not have the training to read logic diagrams or troubleshoot problems. Steps like the example above would verify a cable had indeed been plugged into the correct socket. Second, the manufacturing engineers were verifying that their assembly instructions were correct. As time went on, the instructions were simplified as everyone became more familiar with the machine. Even more simplified instructions without verifications would eventually be sent with the machine since CEs would be fully trained.

Not my job

We discovered a basic difference in cultures between plant people and field people. As mentioned, every assembly step was checked in some way. If some measurement was not within the specification, we were required to call a Test Engineer to check the problem. He would come down, document the problem, find the cause and note the solution. In other words, he did in the plant, what CEs did every day in the field. So, when something was out of spec, plant people dutifully called for a Test Engineer and then they found a chair and some reading material while they waited for the Engineer to show up. That procedure generally netted a 15-30 minute break. It was definitely counter to our field culture where a problem demanded immediate attention.

140

Our experience was that of always being under the gun at customer offices. So the natural CE response at the factory was to find the problem, fix it and then, when the Test Engineer showed up, fill him in on the details. At first, plant people resented our disruption of their routine... and break times. Eventually, we taught each other tricks that benefited both. Overall that plant experience was appreciated as it made all of us better at our jobs.

Print Thickness

It probably sounds silly, but one of the extended tests concerned the thickness of the print on a page. The process of transferring toner and then fusing it to paper was far more complicated than one might think. During the printing process, a laser creates an image of the information to be printed onto a special photoconductive material. The laser actually causes the photoconductor to be charged with tiny points of static electricity. Next the photoconductor is brought in contact with the toner which only sticks to the statically charged areas. When the paper meets the toner, the toner is attracted to (transferred to) the paper from the photoconductor. During the next process step the paper, now with toner in place, is squeezed between two rollers. One of the rollers is heated sufficiently to melt the toner as it proceeds through the rollers. When the printed page emerges, the toner does not soak into the paper like ink. It is fused onto the paper surface in a tiny but measureable thickness.

The print thickness is determined by a number of process factors. In the end, the thickness of the print must be within certain limits. Obviously if the toner is too thin, the characters will be weak or incomplete. It would be like using a worn out printer ribbon. On the other hand, toner that is too thick will not fuse properly and can be scratched off or even flake off as the paper flexes.

We had a very special planer tool to measure the thickness of the print. It worked like a wood plane, except this one removed a fraction of a millimeter of toner on each pass. Several areas across the page were selected. In each area the planer tool would be passed over the print while the number of passes were counted until gaps in the characters appeared. Within the specification meant that all parts of the process were working correctly.

DASD Controller

In early 1979, it was back to San Jose for another temporary assignment. This time it was for a product under development with no decision yet on whether or not it would be produced. I was to work mostly helping the development engineers to debug the control unit for this next generation disk storage subsystem.

The subsystem was announced in mid-1980 and became the 3380 Direct Access Storage Device and 3880 Storage Control Unit. This was a very large storage subsystem and the first disk drives to break the "gigabyte barrier." Each 3380 could store over 2.5 gigabytes of data. It's "density" was 4 times that of previous products and it accessed the data more than twice as fast. The 3380 DASD units could be connected together in strings of 4. The 3880 Control Unit had the ability to control 4 separate strings of 3380s and transfer data to 2 different computers

Inside a 3380 frame.   Photo: Finnish DP Museum Association.

all at the same time. The 3880 Control Unit was the first to include "data caching." The cache was a temporary memory that could hold data until an access path was open. The 3880/3380 combination proved to be IBM's most profitable disk subsystem. It was marketed for 15 years, even though it had been projected to be obsolete in just five years. By today's standards, it was physically huge for such a small capacity, but this was over 35 years ago. Back then it was a major breakthrough.

The assignment consisted mostly of troubleshoot extremely intermittent errors. These were errors that occurred so infrequently that we used special multichannel recording oscilloscopes to capture the failures. Almost every time the error was some sort of timing condition where several things had to happen before the error <u>might</u> occur. Creating the conditions for an error to occur was the major challenge. It was very interesting work, but often boring too, as we waited for an error to occur.

It also resulted in working odd hours, when the two prototype machines were available. One of the engineers I worked with was on a local bowling league, so every Thursday, we did not start work until after his league finished. Flextime was something CEs understood very well.

Liaison

Another type of opportunity presented itself on this assignment. It seems there was a small group of people in San Jose known as Product Test. In their separately secured building, their job was to test every product before it was released to manufacturing. Every aspect of a machine was required to meet the design specifications. And that meant everything. They began with physical dimensions – length, width, height off the floor, the physical placement of casters on the frame. Everything. Anything out of spec stopped the procedure and required correction to match product specification or the justification and approval for a change of that specification. That occasionally required removal of the test machine back to engineering for the solution.

The people in Product Test were very territorial, even anal about any machine in their facility. Each machine had to be located in a separately secured area guarded by infrared sensors and motion detectors. Once testing began, Development Engineers were allowed only escorted entry, to ensure test results were not compromised. My San Jose manager politely put it this way, "The contention system works well in San Jose."

Despite the obvious acrimony, there was still a need to communicate between the organizations. The normal interface was accomplished at the management level. With his project now ramping up, my manager was swamped. He asked me to be the department liaison, calculating that my being an outsider might help ease the normal tension between Development and Product Test. So my badge was updated to allow entry into the sacred halls of the Product Test building.

Mostly the job involved participating in relevant meetings and being a messenger boy. Occasionally things got interesting when the development people wanted to update the product under test. This was allowed only if the update affected a portion of the machine that had not yet been certified or if the change did not alter the specifications. Most often it was a fix for some oddball intermittent problem. At first, product test gave me a hard time about everything. That was their modus operandi. At one particularly contentious meeting, I finally had enough of the nit-picking and said, "You know? I don't really give a hoot if this gets done or not. I'm on a temp assignment from Field Engineering so I could just pack up and go home. Then you people can argue directly with the engineers." After that, they understood not to shoot the messenger.

As a CE, I was also called upon several times to install one of the approved fixes or updates to a test machine. It was just another Engineering Change to me. There was one incident where I was to install an update, but it had to be done on a Sunday morning so that it would not interfere with the scheduled testing.

Come Sunday morning, I found that the security system had not been disabled as prearranged. I informed security of the problem but they said I was not on their schedule. They would need to get approval from a manager before allowing entry to the area. They gave me a name and number to call. I did so and related the story to the duty manager for that day. He agreed to take care of it. About 10 minutes later, I was able to enter the area and proceed with the update.

An hour and a half later, a well-dressed stranger came through the door. I had not expected anyone except a guard making his rounds. I greeted him. He asked how my update was going and offered to buy me a coffee. Turned out he was the manager I spoke with on the phone. In reality, he was a second level manager who took over when the assigned duty manager suddenly took ill.

He decided to stop by after church to see just who he talked with. We talked for quite a while. He seemed genuinely impressed with the variety of experiences that CEs had "out in the field." At one point, he said, "Damn! All I've got is Specialists. What I really need is a Generalist!" After a short pause he added, "But I don't have any slots available." Made my day anyway.

Lunchtime Solutions

The San Jose site was not a traditional factory or plant site at all. It actually was an early version of the so called corporate campus concept. Most of the buildings shared a common mall and relaxation area that was beautifully landscaped. A large reflecting pool contained the signature dynamic sculpture *"Hydro-Gyro"* designed by Robert Boardman Howard in 1958. Surrounding buildings housed various development and research facilities as well as administration and more than a few assembly buildings.

To accommodate the variety of people and strange work hours, a central cafeteria operated 24 hours a day. This offered a chance to rub elbows with some truly remarkable people as well as some strangely interesting individuals. Often we shared tables with engineers from other projects, assemblers, research fellows and the like. There were also foreign engineers here to hone their skills on some new technology or even present papers on some of their own innovations. Problems were sometimes solved in discussions over lunch.

Although the cafeteria contained a variety of table styles, we most often sat at a rectangular table that seated ten or so. Once, at such a table, Tom, a Service Planning Representative from another disk drive project sat down across from me. After eating, Tom took a small manila

San Jose's "Hydro Gyro" Sculpture

envelope from his shirt pocket and proceeded to spread its contents down the middle of the table. Then he sat down and confidently said, "I'll bet you guys don't know what these are." Everyone looked over the ¾" black disks that seemed to be made of a rubbery material. I recognized the disks, having replaced some in the recent past. So I spoke up and said, "Those look like crash stops." His face indicated that his confidence had just departed. Tom looked me straight in the eye and said, "You damn CEs know everything."   When the laughter subsided, he went on to explain that his problem today was really about the material the little disks were made from. He had spent all morning in a very frustrating meeting trying to convince others that they should be made of a different material.   He had lost the battle over the material costs.

This slightly cheaper material had been used in the previous generation disk drives. It was found that the material became sticky after 6-7 years in the heated environment of a disk drive. That led to a problem we called "stiction." It was a serious problem that prevented a disk drive from entering the "ready" state. Although the part was inexpensive, the replacement procedure was quite involved and time consuming. He had lobbied to use a material that lasted at least twice

146

as long for a fraction of a penny more. In reality, his judgment was correct and he eventually won in a later round.

As a Service Planning Representative, Tom's job was to insure that a product would be serviceable in the field. In other words, he looked out for CE interests while products were being developed. I later found that he was also a pocket watch expert. He was a collector of antique pocket watches and a well-known authority in those circles. He had even been called upon as an expert witness in court cases involving authenticity and insurance valuations.

Madman Dave

One fine spring day, I was visiting my friend Mike at his San Jose home. Mike and I had worked together before he transferred to the San Jose site. At one point his wife asked him to make a quick run to the store. I hung out in his garage workshop while he made the 5 minute trip. Shortly after he left, a guy in work clothes came walking up the driveway waving a lawn sprinkler head with a foot long el-shaped piece of plastic pipe attached. He was half mumbling, half cussing about something. Angrily, he asked, "Where's Mike?" I told him Mike had run up to the store and would be back in a minute. He continued his rant, while waving the broken off sprinkler head. It seems the pop-up head had bound up and would not do its thing. He was so frustrated with not being able to free the sticking head that he had ripped it right out of the ground. He finally did introduce himself as Dave, a neighbor.

At first I thought his beef was with the quality of the product. I was wrong. He was cussing out the engineer who designed it. He pointed out that this idiot designed it in such a way that there was brass on brass contact. This stupid so and so should have known better. Brass against brass always binds up. He should have designed it with a nylon insert to prevent such a problem. Mike came back, his task completed. We calmed Dave down and then we helped him free up the sprinkler head and repair his watering system.

Later, Mike told me it was a riot to watch Dave weeding his yard. He would use a hoe to hack away at any weed that dared to invade his grass. The nerve of the damn things. Eccentric yes, but also brilliant. It seems Dave worked at the research facility and held several important patents for disk drive electronic circuitry.

147

Pajaro

By 1989, I definitely knew the way to San Jose. This time the Pajaro project brought me back to California's Silicon Valley. The project name was not chosen as Spanish for bird, but for being a river name. California rivers were being used for project code names at the time. This project was quite different in that it involved an internal "tool" rather than a product destined for customer sale. It involved a series of software programs installed on an IBM PS/2 Personal Computer and designed to help CEs manage large accounts. It allowed real-time hardware monitoring of the customer systems, record keeping and communication capabilities. Eventually Pajaro was given the official name of IBM Service Director/2.

The concept was refined over the years and although the original Service Director/2 was retired years ago, parts of it remain. Some of its service features have been incorporated into hardware products and more recently, IBM brought out a software product for customer use that includes many of the original monitoring and reporting ideas.

I joined the project at a point when a small number of machines were about to be hand built for field testing. We handled the assembly of the required hardware and then loaded the necessary programs, which ran under the OS/2 Operating System. The Service Director was then packed and shipped to selected accounts, along with a booklet of operating instructions. The concept was entirely new and frankly many CEs did not understand its capabilities. On top of that, the software was still a bit shaky. Fortunately for the account CEs, the operating instruction booklets included phone numbers for our project group when questions arose.

The hard drive on each new Service Director received an exact image of all the programs on our "gold" machine. That machine was the standard for all others and contained only the latest tested versions of the necessary programs. That way, we knew nothing was missed and they were always up to date.

As time went on, updates for bug fixes became necessary and another dedicated machine was set up for that task. A set of update diskettes could easily be generated from that machine. And yes, Personal Computers still used diskettes in 1989. Each update only required the inclusion of a "loader" diskette, which contained a set of program instructions called a batch file. The field CE needed only to begin with the loader disk and then follow the on-screen prompts to complete an update.

Difficulties are inevitable on any new product and we had a few. We thought we had the update procedure down cold until one CE called in with a problem. I took the call. It took a goodly while, but we resolved the issue and were about to hang up when suddenly he asked, "Hey, when are you guys going to update the 'ABC' program?" (Sorry but he named a copyrighted PC game, so not the real name.) I questioned, "The 'ABC' program?" He said, "Yea, I know there's a newer version out."

I went into parent mode and began repeating the part where the instructions forbid any private use of the Service Director. He shot back, "Then why the hell did you guys put it there?" Naturally, I denied that accusation. He was insistent that it had to be us because he was the only one in his account with the password to his Service Director. I said I would look into it.

As soon as we hung-up, I headed to our update machine. A program directory that did not belong was soon found. It contained the illicit game. I immediately removed all traces of the program from our machine. The real question was how did it get there? Furthermore, how many of our Service Director machines were affected? As you might guess, there was a round of meetings to discuss the ramifications of illegally distributing software. More importantly, now what?

The resolution was that we wrote a special script for the next update. It included several hidden commands that interrogated the hard drive to determine if the illegal file directory existed. If it did, we silently erased the directory, its contents and all traces of that program. If that directory was not on the system, the script simply continued on its merry way as usual. The updates were sent to all Service Directors in the field. Everything went as planned. We fixed the problem and nobody knew it existed, except that one guy. He called in about a week after the update went out. He was hopping mad. "Why the hell did you guys erase my game?" All I could say was, "sorry, just doing our job."

Eventually we did find the culprit. It was a security guard. In making his rounds, he saw a machine just sitting there. So, he brought the game from home to play during those moments when things were a little too quiet. He did not realize that by playing the game, he actually installed it on our special purpose machine.

Not done yet

When 1991 rolled around, all the Service Director/2 component programs had all been written and most bugs had been removed. San Jose was ready to roll out SD/2 machines to all accounts with mainframe computers. I found myself back in San Jose for 6 months to set up a Support Center for the Service Director/2. At first I would be a support center of one. After setup and the kinks worked out, other CEs would be called in to help. Eventually, after the rollout was completed, the Pajaro Project would end and our function would be transferred to the National Service Support Centers.

Fortunately I had saved most of my notes on various problems and fixes from the earlier assignment. That was a start. The new support center was an office almost large enough for two people when carefully arranged. They brought in desks, chairs and storage cabinets. A Service Director was installed so we could simulate problems if necessary. Naturally, there were PCs available that connected to internal systems. And, what would a support center be without telephones and headsets.

It was a cozy setup right in the middle of all the Pajaro Project people. Many resources were available just steps away. In addition, we had access to secure internal databases like a list of the SD/2 locations and details. I also managed to develop an in-house symptom/fix database that could be instantly updated from our terminals.

Two doors down the hall to the right was our documentation specialist. Al was responsible for every bit of paper associated with SD/2. He wrote all the installation instructions, operating manuals, tech manuals, update sheets, etc. He had been a software engineer, so he understood the need for good documentation. Early on, the phones did not ring that often, so I got to wander around and chat with my neighbors. Soon Al began showing up at my door with document folders. He decided that since I came from the field, I would make the perfect sounding board for his documentation. Initially there was plenty of time, so I read over what he had written and offered my thoughts. It quickly became obvious that programmers and hardware people spoke different languages. Usually it only took a minute or two to agree on some rewording. But at times, it was a learning experience for both of us. It was a great example of the complications in producing any new product or service.

SD/2 Support Center in San Jose

Whenever a batch of SD/2s shipped, a rise in calls could be expected three to four days later. As volume increased, we added one, then two more temporary CEs to the group. Not every CE had the temperament for telephone troubleshooting. Remember, CEs were basically hands-on type people – computer mechanics. More than one CE passed through our doors in both directions.

As my departure date neared, I got a call from my manager back home. Following protocol, San Jose had asked permission to keep me another 6 months. On this assignment, I had come alone since my wife was working as a tutor for a local college. We had had monthly trips and she came for an extended stay during the summer. But I was anxious to catch-up and straighten up around my home and yard before winter set in. We settled on a 3 month extension.

The next three months went well. By October, my replacement was ready and I headed back to my former life in the field. My previous accounts had long since been assigned to others so I became a CE at large. That turned out to be a good thing.

Remote Control

Around Thanksgiving, my San Jose manager was back in the picture. It seems the planned transfer of the Service Director to the National Support Center had not happened. Since the Service Director was mostly software based, NSC did not have the people to handle such software support. They needed time to get some of their people properly trained. So much for planning.

A deal was forged between San Jose and my office. Cleveland would supply an office, telephones and me. San Jose would supply the equipment and a dollar two-ninety-eight to cover costs. Phones were set up so I could take support calls directly and I had direct phone and digital access to San Jose. Basically we had the same resources as before, so for all intents and purposes, I was in San Jose. Only a few of us knew the truth. To my knowledge, that was the first time such a remote support center had been created.

My assignment continued until about May of 1992 when our National Support Center was finally able to take over. Then it was back to the "old grind." It was time. Like pilots, Customer Engineers disliked flying a desk.

Beginning with the Commodore PET in 1977, the market for micro-computers (as they were first called) blossomed. Companies like Apple, Radio Shack and Amiga became household names. At first, these desktop size computers were viewed as toys for nerds or Yuppies who just had to have the latest and greatest.

Almost missing the sales boat, IBM did not introduce its 5150 Personal Computer until 1981. With that announcement came the notion that these small computers were not toys after all. In spite of being named a personal computer, IBM marketed its machines mostly to businesses as companions that would lighten the workload on mainframe computers. Other manufacturers latched onto the name personal computer and took up marketing them to consumers. The machines had evolved from micro-computers to home computers. The goal was a computer in every home. Of course it's obvious that goal was met and exceeded many times over.

Shrinking machines

Shortly after the IBM PC hit the market, changes could be seen in the entire data processing industry. The mainframe computers were still king and dominated the business world, but they too were beginning to shrink not only in size, but also in power requirements and price. At the same time, all computers, mainframes on down continued to increase their capabilities. Soon "mini-computers" like Digital Equipment Corporation's PDP Series became as powerful as older mainframes. And Personal computers were becoming as powerful as mini computers.

To me, the perfect example of the technological advances of those times can be seen in the differences between the IBM System 360 Model 40 and the IBM PC Jr. Don't laugh until you read the rest of my story. The time span was only 18 years. Introduced in 1965, the System 360/40 was capable of running entire businesses. The IBM PC Jr. of 1983 was the smallest, least powerful computer IBM ever made.

It was a System 360 model 40 which was Cleveland State University's first mainframe computer. That machine ran the entire university. Standard business applications like accounts receivable and payable, payroll plus student records, grades and scheduling. And still there was time available to run jobs submitted by students in the various programming courses.

A typical System 360 Model 40 installation

The PC Jr. arrived on the scene with an advertising campaign featuring "The Lil' Tramp." It was aimed squarely at the home market. The playful advertising campaign made it sound like a toy rather than a serious computer. Yet in many ways it included more features than its slightly older brother, the 5150 Personal Computer. For instance, the PC jr. featured the first wireless computer keyboard. It included a built-in game cartridge slot. It had video graphics and several other features.

Yet the tech media soundly vilified it for lack of features and even ridiculed the PC jr. for its "chicklet style" keyboard. In reality the keyboard was way ahead of its time. Today almost all computer keyboards use this same technology. Many keyboards are now wireless as well. The poor ad campaign and intense negative publicity forced the PC jr.'s market withdrawal in less than 2 years.

IBM PC jr. Home Computer. Notice the size of the mouse.

Despite the flop of the PC Jr., the technological advances in 18 years compared to the System 360/40 were nothing short of amazing. Those changes are obvious in the following comparisons.

	System 360/Model 40	IBM PC jr.
Approx. physical size	60" x 31" x 60"h	14" x 11.5" x 4"h
Physical volume	64.6 cu. ft.	0.37 cu .ft.

Memory

Memory speed	2.5ms	1.15ms
System max. memory	256k	512k
Size of add-on memory	62" x 26" x 70"h	11.5" x 4" x 1.5"

(The 360/40 required an additional frame vs. a "memory slice")

Features

Input device	modified typewriter	wireless keyboard
Output device	modified typewriter	color monitor
Graphics capability	none	16 color graphics
Sound capability	alarm bell	yes + game effects
Joysticks ports	you're kidding	2
Game cartridges	still kidding right?	1

The size reduction was phenomenal. Doing the math shows that 175 PC Jr.'s would physically fit inside the 360/40 frame. Notice that additional memory for the 360/40 meant adding another complete frame. The additional frame more than doubled the size of the 360/40 due to requirements for additional power supplies necessary for the old "core" type memory. Technmical advances shrunk memory size much faster than anything else. Believe it or not, over 1,600 of the PC jr. "memory slices" would have fit inside that added 360/40 memory frame! You may have also noted the PC Jr. memory capacity was actually twice that of the 360/40.

The largest difference between mainframes and PCs was in the way peripheral equipment (input and output devices) were attached. Mainframe computers could add hundreds of peripherals due to hardware known as a "channel." Each channel was designed to handle as many as 256 input/output or storage devices. And even the smallest mainframe included a minimum of three channels. Personal Computers have been limited to only a few peripherals or attachments. And the newer, handheld tablet computers are extremely limited when it comes to peripherals.

Despite the advantage of channels, mainframe computers were <u>almost</u> made obsolete. Large computers are still with us in the form of servers and super-computers. While their size remains comparatively large, the insides, the architecture is very different. Super computers now contain literally hundreds or even thousands of smaller computers all connected to work together. "Deep Blue," the famous chess playing computer from 1996 is an example of such a machine. Another is "Watson" which competed on the TV game show *"Jeopardy!"* and now is doing medical research.

Something many people do not realize is that, in a way, mainframe computers caused their own demise. Really. Computers have always been used for research, even from the very beginning. So it is their research that led to the breakthroughs large and small that allowed this shrinking of technology.

ET phone home

In the 1982 movie "E.T. the Extra-Terrestrial," the young boy, Elliott, helps build a device to allow the stranded E.T. to "phone home." That was fiction. It took real computers more than a decade to accomplish that same feat. The RAMAC 2 Array Subsystem was IBM's first large RAID-5 disk storage system and it actually phoned home.

The term RAID stands for 'redundant array of independent disks.' That's nerd talk for a special way of storing information to protect the data against a hardware failure. There are a number of ways to accomplish that goal. The RAID-5 system uses sets of 4 independent disk drives of the same type and size as used in personal computers. Data is split into 3 "stripes" (pieces of the data). The stripes are stored on 3 separate disk drives. From those 3 stripes, a fourth stripe called the "parity block" is created and stored on the 4th disk drive. If any one of the disk drives were to fail, the other 3 can be used to recreate the missing data. It may sound like magic, but it is not. It is a combination of hardware and software that gets the job done.

Here is a much simplified example of how it works:

1 - For our data, we'll use just the word "ace."
2 - Splitting this data into stripes would place the "a" on disk 1, the "c" on disk 2 and the "e" on disk 3.

3 - To create the 4th stripe, the parity block, we need to assign a value to each letter. For that purpose, we will assign the number equal to each letter's position in the alphabet.
    a=1, c=3, e=5
4 - The parity block value will be the result of the formula:
    pb = 1+3+5.
5 - The 4th disk would therefore contain a stripe with the value 9.

Now, with that data in place, let's create an error. Suddenly the second disk drive stops working. Kaput! The available data stripes would be:
    disk1 = a, **disk 2 = ?,** disk 3 = e, disk 4 = 9

To recover the missing data, we simply apply the same formula we used for building the parity block(#4 above). 9 = 1 + ? + 5

So the missing data is calculated to be '3' or the third letter of the alphabet, "c".

Naturally there is far more to it than the example, but the point is the missing data can actually be recreated using simple mathematics. This is done in the disk control unit in real time and the computer system would never see a problem. At some later time that bad disk drive can be replaced. Then, using special software in the control unit, all the missing data from the bad disk drive can be rewritten to the new disk. Amazing technology. A disk drive broke, but the computer never knew it happened.

The rest of the story

So how did that bad disk drive actually get replaced? Easy. Remember we said this machine was capable of phoning home. The failure was recognized and an error code was generated by the control circuitry. The error code and other information about the machine were automatically phoned in to a service reporting center. There, computers analyzed the code and a list of likely defective parts was generated. The machine ID produced the customer name and the assigned CE was notified of the problem. The list of suspected parts allowed the CE to pick up those parts on his way to the customer location. After the replacement was made and testing completed, the CE initiated a built-in program that rebuilds the missing data. He was then free to leave. The machine completed the rebuilding of the data during its spare time. The wonders of technology.

No longer necessary was the highly trained Customer Engineer. As new technology continued to reduce the need for CEs, I was reminded of the prediction made during my initial training back in 1966. "During your careers, the only constant will be change. And in all likelihood, your job will disappear before you retire." And so the end of the "mainframe mechanic" began.

Downsizing

As the need for highly trained Customer Engineers declined, other changes were taking place in the business world. The change from a "Personnel Department" to "Human Resources" signaled the change in corporate attitude. The Field Engineering Division was among the last employers still adhering to Theory Y. Employee contributions had always been appreciated and employees were treated with respect. But now, something had to be done about the excess number of employees.

Initial downsizing attempts featured bonuses of 2 years' salary to those willing to take early retirement. Other benefits such as retraining for a post-retirement career were also offered. Those nearing 65 could not afford to pass up such an opportunity. To those 60 and over, it was for serious consideration.

Still there remained excess CEs. This was due mostly to the hiring binge of the mid-60s These people were still in their fifties and could not afford to stretch even an extra 2 years pay to reach the minimum Social Security age of 62. Relentlessly the pressure to leave continued despite progressively shrinking offers. Down to a one year bonus. Then only a six month bonus.

The End is Near

The next change came with the demise of the Field Engineering Division. The corporate reasoning was that technology was making hardware much more reliable, so the thinning of the service ranks was inevitable. Millions of dollars could be saved by eliminating the separate organization. All FE personnel were folded into the Sales

Division. The Sales Division was happy. Those remaining CEs could provide sales leads. Corporate leaders had always known that customers trusted their CEs far more than the sales people.

Sales people have the saying, "Nothing happens until you sell something." CEs had a saying too, "We work for the company, salesmen work for themselves." The first statement cannot be denied. Neither can the second. The latter is based on the way each was compensated. CEs, as with other employees, were salaried, but salesmen worked on salaries plus commission. An important distinction.

The loss of a distinct service division brought an immediate change in the attitude of management. The old Field Engineering people had always been driven by challenge and pride of accomplishment. Money was a secondary reward. It was never necessary to dangle dollar bills in front of a CE for motivation.

Of course the sales people were driven by money. Their commission. The Sales Division tried all sorts of marketing ploys to convert CEs into sales resources. CEs were offered rewards for sales leads. Not commissions mind you. Those were reserved for sales people. These rewards were small cash amounts for "leads" that resulted in sales. It was much like the cell phone company that offers you $10 off your next bill if you recommend someone who actually signs up for their service.

Whenever office-wide meetings were held, it was at a banquet hall, not a local church basement or the office cafeteria. At these meetings, seemingly random gift certificates or cash awards of perhaps $100 would be handed out. Of course old computer mechanics were not impressed. Remember that story about the straw hat and cane? To a man, Customer Engineers hated the whole concept and became very vocal about it. Fearing open rebellion, management retreated from that tactic.

Still the shift to Theory X continued. Soon the emphasis became the employee's "contribution to the bottom line" rather than an outstanding job. In other words, it was still about money rather than accomplishment. The carrots still dangled, but now there was a stick attached. Rather than raises, bonuses would be awarded to the "best" office. Customer Engineers and other former Field Engineering people had little difficulty in realizing their labors had little, if anything, to do with revenue.

Various programs began popping up to aid in reducing the workforce. What had been an annual pay raise (unless you really messed up), became a drought of several years, perhaps followed by a meager raise. Another corporate change capped retirement earnings at 30 years. Previously, employees continued to earn increases in retirement though years of service, etc.

Still another program, which was considered by many to be Gestapo tactics, instituted a rating system where each employee was to write a critique of the other members of their team or department. Part of the critique was a required section labeled "suggestions for individual improvement." The push toward the door was obvious. Many CEs had 30 years of service but were too young for Social Security. They remained trapped due to age.

Management personnel were not immune to the pressures. Head counts had to be reduced and managers were required to meet the numbers or lose their jobs. The whole system rapidly deteriorated to simple self-preservation. With fear for your job, the shift to Theory X was complete.

After close to 33 years with the company and still under 60 years old, this Mainframe Mechanic was forced to call it quits. The retirement package included 6 months' salary which, supplemented with savings and some part-time work would allow us to hold out until Social Security kicked in. It was a relief from the pressure exerted on us "old-timers."

It was also a very sad time. The hundreds of customer people we came to know over the years. The dozens and dozens of people we had known well and worked alongside. The socializing with the many great people who had become close friends. But it was time to go. The mainframe era had passed. The job had evolved and vanished. There was no longer a need for mainframe mechanics.

18 - Epilogue

Another World

There truly was a world of difference between the beginning of the mainframe era and its fade into history. The technological changes had been predicted. Yet the machines had changed and shrunk far more than expected. The business environment had changed in many unexpected ways. Despite the way the end unfolded, the mainframe era was a unique golden sliver of technological history. Its mechanics continued to fade a little with each new technological breakthrough and new product. In a generation the whole Mainframe Era will be ancient history, if not already. The old computer mechanics began disappearing before the turn of the 21st Century. Time, technology and business march on.

Except for the last few years of hanging on, it was a career to be proud of. During the Mainframe Era, CEs worked hard and played hard. It was definitely not the boredom of an assembly line.

By the way, most of us knew the difference. I had a factory job once (and only once.) I manned a machine that cut long copper extrusions into segments for making electric motor commutators. The first day was OK. On the second day boredom began to set in and I found myself silently calculating my productivity. How many commutator segments per Extrusion? Per hour? Per day? Shortly after noon on the third day I was asked to work several hours overtime that night. My ultimate boredom level had been reached. I quit on the spot. On the other hand, CEs never found their job to be boring. Never.

For the most part, change had been a CE's friend. There was always something new and interesting. Every new machine that was announced meant something to be learned and a new challenge. Every computer hiccup was an opportunity to think, to reason, to use your skills and to learn new ones. That commencement speaker way back at Basic School was so right! His predictions all came true, even the one about the job being gone before retirement.

When people retire, they often say they miss the job. They miss the daily routine. I believe every Customer Engineer would disagree for two reasons. First, of course, the job no longer existed. Those of us who experienced the Mainframe Era began mourning its decay in the 1990s. Secondly, there was no daily routine. As Forrest Gump might have put it, every day was a box of chocolates. All in a good way.

People Not Machines

The continuous technological change of the day was exciting, but the predominant memories are of the people, not the machines. It was constant amazement of the intelligence and knowledge of the people surrounding us. Their depth and diversity of personality. So many with totally different lives away from the job. The home designer/builder. The many musicians. The drag racer. The bikers, motorized and pedaled. The amateur astronomer. The pilots (more than one of those too). The pocket watch expert. The bowlers and softball players. The refugee engineer who did his own butchering as well as everything else.

There was the manager with the photographic memory who could quote word for word what you said a year earlier. The parts room guy who remembered every Customer Engineer in the city and the entire parts inventory. And the unforgettable secretary (Executive Assistant if you prefer), who knew exactly where everybody and everything was located at any given time. She was a real live version of Radar from M.A.S.H.

The customer people we knew were no less amazing. The computer operator who was a genuine professional student. The psychologist turned Data Processing Manager. The Computer Room Supervisor who had a new Polish joke ready every single day. No exceptions. All these kept the mainframe mechanic's job interesting.

Life Goes On

The horse and buggy days are gone. Soon self-driving cars will be parked in the garage. The mainframe computers are gone along with their mechanics. Already we converse with Star-Trek like handheld communicators we call cell phones. Life goes on.

The mainframe mechanics, the Customer Engineers, of old are gone too. But not that far. If you keep your eyes and ears open, you'll find them. Old CEs (and often their spouses) still gather to talk about the good old days. Early in the morning on the first Monday of the month, check that round table at the back of the restaurant. Or maybe it will be on the second Tuesday of the month. Check that group of a dozen or so noisy old men and women in the corner of the restaurant on Wednesday evening. If you listen in on their conversations, you just might hear references to archaic computer terms like "CPU" or "old gray iron." Or perhaps you'll hear the term "call out." Possibly even "mainframe mechanic."

References

For those interested in learning more about the world of mainframe computers, the following offer much more information, photographs and videos.

http://www.computerhistory.org/revolution/topics
http://www.demorton.com/Tech/$OSTL.pdf
http://en.wikipedia.org/wiki/History_of_IBM
http://www-03.ibm.com/history

Images acknowledgement
Images not individually credited were obtained from one of the following:

Author's personal photos and reference material
IBM historic publications
IBM online archives

The Data Communication System in Chapter 7
More information can be found in an IBM promotional video for the DCS. It has been saved on YouTube at:

https://www.youtube.com/watch?v=FkKUACR0UYU

Some noteworthy images are found on this video at approximately the following times:
1:20 - The Operator Console of a System 360/30
3:36 - An open CE "tool bag" on the console table.
-

River references in Chapter 8
The broad flat banks of the Cuyahoga River were home to many heavy industries despite the hazards of its navigating its meandering course. The name Collision Bend was not given. It just sort of happened as ships collided with each other or the river bank. Actually, this infamous bend in the river was the inspiration that led to the invention of the "bow thruster" which is now standard on almost all large ships. A short YouTube film about the bend is available at:

https://www.youtube.com/watch?v=_zYlJYtG_UQ

Also search on "images of collision bend".

Enjoy!